Irene Howat has the unique gift of listening, and the ability to take what is heard and, out of her wise, compassionate and godly spirit, produce literature that challenges and encourages those who read it.

Nothing takes God by surprise. He knows the plans he has for each one of us (Jeremiah 29:11), and the varied experiences in our lives are all part of his heart's desire to conform us to the image of his beloved Son. As you read the stories of the men and women in this book, you cannot but see that although each walks with God, their experiences are very different. But there is a thread that runs through all of their stories, the thread of suffering. God has used this to mature them and make them what they are today, not survivors, but overcomers.

God's Word tells us much about suffering, and why we experience it. He uses it to refine our faith, to produce character. Suffering disciplines us and it brings glory to God. It also keeps us from going astray, and teaches us the faith. Following God's statutes are le_____ to Hebrews tells u_____ple is the Sufferin_____st, 'Although he w_____ience from what he suffered (Hebrews 5:8).

In this book you will find these truths expressed by those who have known the Refiner's fire in their lives. May their stories, sensitively and compassionately compiled and edited by Irene, who is no stranger to suffering, inspire and be a blessing to all who read it.

Jessie McFarlane

DEDICATION

For my brothers and their families

Anchored in the Storm

edited by Irene Howat

Christian Focus

Christian Focus Publications publishes biblically-accurate books for adults and children. The books in the adult range are published in three imprints.

Christian Heritage contains classic writings from the past.

Christian Focus contains popular works including biographies, commentaries, doctrine, and Christian living.

Mentor focuses on books written at a level suitable for Bible College and seminary students, pastors, and others; the imprint includes commentaries, doctrinal studies, examination of current issues, and church history.

For a free catalogue of all our titles, please write to
Christian Focus Publications,
Geanies House, Fearn,
Ross-shire, IV20 1TW, Great Britain

For details of our titles visit us on our web site
http://www.christianfocus.com

© Christian Focus Publications

ISBN 185792 656 0

Published in 2001 by
Christian Focus Publications
Geanies House, Fearn, Ross-shire
IV20 1TW, Great Britain

Cover design by Owen Daily

Contents

ACKNOWLEDGEMENT 6

CONTRIBUTORS 7

1. GWEN MacDOUGALL 13

2. KEITH WESTON 29

3. BERTIE AND PAT JOHNSTON 43

4. HOPE SCOTT 57

5. AJITH FERNANDO 67

6. VALERIE SMITH 83

7. PETER TRUMPER 97

8. JIM AND MARGARET PRESCOTT . 115

9. ROB HOPKINS 129

10. EMMA FARAGHER 145

11. SANDY FINLAYSON 163

12. EFFIE LAMONT 177

ACKNOWLEDGEMENT

It is a costly business to share difficult experiences, especially in print. Private things become public, and strangers who read what you have written know more about you than do some of your friends. But the contributors to this book have been prepared to do that because as they faced problems and challenges in their lives they found God faithful to his promise to be with them, even when sometimes they could not feel his presence. And they have been prepared to share their experiences in order that those who read this book will be encouraged in their faith in Jesus Christ, and challenged if they don't already know him as their Saviour and Friend.

I wish to thank the contributors for their courage and for the privilege of working with them.

Irene Howat

CONTRIBUTORS

GWEN MacDOUGALL

Gwen and her husband Dave had two children, Ruth and Ewan. Ruth had just begun secondary school in their home city of Dundee, when she became ill with what was discovered to be cancer. Treatment followed, but Ruth died when she was just twelve years old. Ruth was a very special girl; even as a patient undergoing treatment for her cancer she was concerned to help the other children in Yorkhill Hospital, Glasgow. After her daughter's death, Gwen set up Ruth's Yorkhill Fund which raised over £65,000 before it was finally closed.

KEITH WESTON

Born in 1926, Keith Weston first understood that Jesus died for him at a wartime Christian Harvest Camp when he was eleven years old. Four years of army service led to Cambridge and ordination in 1953. Keith was Rector of a large Oxford church for twenty-one years, reaching out to many students over that time. In 1991 he retired. For three years Keith Weston was Chairman of the Keswick Convention, and he has spoken at many similar conventions all over the world. He is married to Margaret, and they have four married children, all in Christian service.

BERTIE AND PAT JOHNSTON

Bertie Johnston and his wife Pat live in Dungannon in Northern Ireland. Brought up on a farm in Co. Fermanagh, Bertie sought his fortune in Manchester, returning home penniless after a year. Soon afterwards he met Pat, and months later they were both converted. Bertie served in the Royal Ulster Constabulary, in the CID and Regional Crime Squad, for ten years. For most of his service, he was dealing with terrorism. Often in danger, Bertie and Pat were forced to rely on the Lord for their safety from day to day. Bertie Johnston now runs the Lifeboat Mission in Moy.

HOPE SCOTT

Born during the First World War, Hope Scott was reared in the twenties and remembers the hardships of the Depression years. She and her husband Tom were at the stage of bringing up their own children when Tom started to have problems with his balance. What began as a nuisance developed into a debilitating illness from which he died. Sadly, as the years passed, it became clear that this was a genetic condition and that future generations might be affected. One of their children has died of it, and grandchildren are affected too.

AJITH FERNANDO

Ajith Fernando and his wife and children live in Sri Lanka, a country that has seen many violent uprisings in the last twenty years. Over 60,000 people have died as a result of the troubles. In his work with Youth for Christ, Ajith has met many difficult and dangerous situations, some of which he shares with readers. Bringing up children in a civil-war situation results in stresses most can't imagine, but Ajith and his wife have decided that for the time being they should remain in Sri Lanka, giving their children a happy and secure home amidst the turmoil that surrounds them.

VALERIE SMITH

Valerie and David Smith live in Co. Durham. David works away from home, returning each weekend. As a result, most of the care of their two daughters, Jennifer and Kathryn, has fallen to Valerie. From nursery school years Jennifer's behaviour had given cause for concern, but it took until she was in her mid teens for a firm diagnosis of autism to be made. Jennifer, a helpful girl and talented artist, has gone through difficult and frustrating times, and these have reflected on the life of her family. She attends a school for autistic students in Sunderland.

PETER TRUMPER

Dr Peter Trumper served congregations in Wales for nearly twenty-five years, before he retired from pastoral work in 1986 because of ill health. Having several times ministered to people with multiple sclerosis, he found himself suffering from the same disease. Since retirement, Peter has founded Vocal Protestants' International Fellowship, and is editor of its journal *1521*. He is also the author of several books. Peter and his wife Margaret have four children and six grandchildren. They live in Holywell, North Wales.

JIM AND MARGARET PRESCOTT

The Prescotts come from Glasgow, but they have served the Lord as Salvation Army Officers in London, Findochty in the north-east of Scotland, their native Glasgow, and Campbeltown in Argyll. Not long after moving to Campbeltown, Jim was hospitalized. His mother had died of cancer, and it seemed that the same disease might have struck her son. There were some difficult days to be gone through with the support of the Campbeltown folk, and of their son and daughter, Richard and Morag. Following surgery Jim made a good recovery.

ROB HOPKINS

An only child, Rob Hopkins was converted as a young man. When he and his wife Helen moved 400 miles from his parents, they went to live nearby. Over the years that followed, Rob's father developed cancer and dementia. Caring for him was a steep learning curve. Not long after his father died, Rob's mother showed early signs of Alzheimer's. The years after that were hard, coping with teenaged children and an increasingly confused and frustrated old lady. Rob's mother, who is now blessed with peace, lives in a home near her son and daughter-in-law.

EMMA FARAGHER

After a happy and fulfilled childhood near Plymouth in Devon, Emma Faragher moved to Durham to attend university there. Before the end of her first year, Emma was crippled by back pain and had to rely on her friends to cater for all her needs. After a day of prayer and fasting in her home church, Emma had a time of healing. However, not long into her second year the pain returned with a vengeance. She attended a month-long pain management programme and since then has been able to better live with her problem. She is newly married to James, a man with an evangelist's heart.

SANDY FINLAYSON

The Finlayson family come from Toronto in Canada. Sandy is Library Director of Tyndale College and Seminary, and Linda works in the library too. Their son Ian makes sure they don't spend all their time among books! Sandy, who was born with spina bifida, is very mobile in his wheelchair. Over the years he has had to face big questions regarding disability and God's power to heal. Sandy and Linda, who met when he was a volunteer in the library in which she worked, are active members of a Presbyterian church in Toronto.

EFFIE LAMONT

Brought up in Strathspey, Effie went to Edinburgh to study. After her marriage to Calum Lamont they made their home in Glenelg, another beautiful part of highland Scotland. The Lamonts were blessed with three sons. Tragically, twenty-two-month-old Peter drowned just eight weeks after his twin brothers, Ronald and Donald, were born. And soon after their silver wedding, Effie was to bear another bitter blow. On a trip to the Holy Land to celebrate God's goodness to them in twenty-five years of married life, Calum suffered a massive stroke and died. Effie, a teacher, has found God faithful to all his promises, even in the darkest days.

1

GWEN MacDOUGALL

'Bye, Mum, see you at lunchtime.' These words accompanied a hug from our eleven-year-old daughter, Ruth, as she sped out the door to begin her secondary education. We had no way of knowing that these days would be few. Eight days later, a severe stomach pain resulted in antibiotics being prescribed and Ruth having a week off school. When the pain did not ease, a second opinion was sought in hospital. A scan was done and a mass, thought to be a cyst, detected. Surgery followed, during which an ovary was removed. Cancer – doesn't that word often startle us? Ruth had cancer. Arrangements were made for her to have chemotherapy at Yorkhill Hospital for Sick Children in Glasgow.

My reaction to that very unexpected news was to give it immediately into God's hands, and that night the Lord granted me a peaceful sleep. Before visiting Ruth the following day, I wrote letters to friends, sharing our news and asking for their support in prayer. Hebrews 13:8 tells us that 'Jesus Christ is the same yesterday and today and forever', and I firmly believed that just as our Lord had healed many people while on earth, he was able to heal Ruth through the power of his Holy Spirit. Fear never entered my heart for a minute, and the peace I experienced was shared by Ruth herself.

I wish it was me
The following six months held a mixture of joy and sorrow. Because we were together twenty-four hours each day I saw even more clearly than before what a wonderful daughter Ruth was. Although her treatment could be very daunting at times, seeing how God helped her to cope was an inspiration. But oh, how I wished it was me lying in that bed. After four visits to Yorkhill, Ruth got the 'all clear' in December, and we thanked and praised God together. During a fifth visit, advised by Ruth's professor, 'just to be on the safe side', my daughter caught chickenpox from a nurse who was carrying the virus.

My husband, Dave, and our seven-year-old son, Ewan, had been with us on that fifth visit as it was during the school Christmas holiday. Dave and Ewan were given accommodation at Yorkhill House, a home for families of patients which was situated just a few hundred metres from the hospital. During previous visits, Ewan lived with friends in Dundee and Dave held the fort at home. Although Ewan knew that Ruth was unwell, because of his age he was not aware of the seriousness of her illness, but with childlike faith believed that God was healing his sister. Despite living apart at these trying times, God gave each of us the strength we required.

Grace sufficient

Ruth's chickenpox resulted in her having to spend a week, which included 16th January 1987, her twelfth and last birthday, in the infectious diseases hospital in Dundee. Over and over again that week I wished that Ruth had caught chickenpox in early primary school like most of her class. Having her hospitalized over her birthday was hard to bear, especially as a much-looked-forward to weekend with friends from Edinburgh had to be postponed. Paul wrote, 'My grace is sufficient for you' (2 Corinthians 12:9) and that week we knew again the truth of it as God graciously kept us all in his loving care. Ruth's parting words to us on her birthday evening were, 'It's exciting having a birthday in hospital.' They brought tears to my eyes. What a daughter!

A few days after Ruth was discharged, while washing the breakfast dishes, I fainted. Our doctor visited and suggested I was just tired out and that I should spend the rest of the day resting on the settee. Ruth was so upset, blaming herself for my tiredness. The Lord, however, gave me the right words to assure her that this was not the case. So that day our roles were reversed. God cared for me through Ruth, who was a picture of love and concern. She was kindly adamant that I obeyed the doctor's instruction, and she looked after me wonderfully well to make sure I did. Thanks to her ministrations, I was back to normal the next day.

'Mum, where is Jesus?'

Ruth was allowed to return to school for three or four half-days the following week. Unfortunately, after only two, the agonizing pain returned. She was taken to hospital in Dundee, but the doctors there could not find the cause of the pain. They thought her upset might have been caused by apprehension at starting school again after such a long absence. This saddened me deeply, both because they had seen Ruth's strength and courage over several months, and because I knew she could not wait to get back to school to see all her friends. Her only fear was that she might have to repeat first year. One night, when we were talking together at home, Ruth asked, 'Mum, where is Jesus?' Although we both knew that the Lord was with us, it was at that moment hard to believe. Like Ruth, I felt deserted, almost abandoned. But the Lord never leaves us at the bottom of the pit. The Apostle Paul's words kept coming to mind: 'I am convinced that neither death nor life, neither angels nor demons, neither the present nor the future, nor any powers, neither height nor depth, nor anything else in all creation, will be able to separate us from the love of God that is in Christ Jesus our Lord' (Romans 8:38-39).

Dave and I clung to those verses. As the result of a scan, a return visit to Yorkhill by ambulance was arranged for the following day, Friday 27th February. On arrival there I was very upset because there was no bed in the ward prepared for Ruth. After sitting on a chair doubled up in pain for over two hours a bed was eventually made up for her in a bay. The relief I felt for my darling daughter was intense. That was the first and last upset I experienced in all our hospital visits. David and Ewan came through that evening and once more were given beds in Yorkhill House. Because of the severity of Ruth's condition they did not return after the weekend. Two days later, after Ruth went into a coma, a Chinese boy's father offered to let us have his son's room if the staff would permit it. The kind man explained that, as they lived in Glasgow, they did not need the use of a room with a parent's bed in it. Ruth was moved into Chi's room that afternoon. Isn't God so very good? Amidst all this I found it upsetting to see Ruth's professor, whom we had all grown to love, surprised and upset at the most recent scan results. But, despite all I was seeing happening,

I still believed from the bottom of my heart that the Lord was healing our dear daughter.

With Jesus

When we were told five days later that Ruth had only twelve to twenty-four hours to live, I still believed that God was going to heal her, but I did pray, 'Dear Father God, if you are to take Ruth, please take her quickly.' With tears in my eyes I told Ewan the news later that day after he returned from an outing with a friend of our minister. Ewan said, 'Don't cry, Mum, Ruth will be with Jesus.' Ewan's calmness did us good. The Lord took Ruth home three hours later. I was stunned. Even when we left Ruth I was numb. I still could hardly begin to believe what had happened. Time seemed to stand still. But after phone calls to Dundee to share the news with our parents and close friends, and many prayers being raised as a result, God's strength returned.

'Why, Lord?'

I thought the Lord would heal Ruth on earth, but he chose to heal her in heaven, and his ways are always right. The day after Ruth died, a friend reminded me of Isaiah's words in 55:8-9: '"For my thoughts are not your thoughts, neither are your ways my ways," declares the Lord. "As the heavens are higher than the earth, so are my thoughts than your thoughts." ' A few weeks later God helped me understand that if he had healed Ruth on earth, as I was sure he was doing for his glory, most people would have believed that healing had come through medical treatment alone.

Although many wept at the funeral, the atmosphere in the church was peaceful and victorious. Our minister, who had known Ruth for some years, referred to her as a special gift, special, but not perfect, as was clear a little later when he mentioned her slight impatience when I could not interpret sign language as quickly as she signed! (I am totally deaf.) Although our hearts were broken, the strength of the Lord and his victory over death were incredibly real. He gave us peace. We knew that Ruth's months of suffering were over, and that she was now with Jesus whom she loved. The Lord gave me such strength that, when a few friends who were visibly upset came to visit, I prayed with them and they too received God's peace. How good he is.

For several weeks I went to our bedroom every Wednesday at 9.00 pm, the day and time Ruth died, and relived the whole event. Tears came and I hurt. So often I asked myself, Why did God take Ruth and leave me? She had so much more to give, she had her whole life in front of her, and me with my deafness making me feel such a nuisance – why did he not take me? One evening a few months later I recall suddenly shouting out to God, 'Why have you done this to me?' That only happened once. Who am I to question the Lord? But I knew he wanted me to pour out my heart to him, and I did.

The next few months held a variety of experiences. I found it odd that amazingly little things could be so hard. For example, on noticing that the expiry date on a packet of biscuits in Marks & Spencer's was January 16th, Ruth's birthday, I could not stop the tears and had to hurry home from town. Another day I saw what looked like, from the rear, a mother and her teenage daughter. My tears flowed as I imagined what shopping outings with Ruth might have been like. I didn't feel bitter, just distressed. Again I had to make a hasty retreat from town. And once, when I saw a lady with a tiny amount of wispy hair indicating that she was undergoing chemotherapy, Ruth's hair falling out came to mind and I felt so sad. When these things happened, I had to take myself to prayer and pour out my hurts and sadness to the Lord.

Practical prayer

I was not the only one who was learning about prayer. A few months after Ruth died, Ewan and his friend Brian were playing football in our back garden. Suddenly Ewan rushed into the house.

'Mum,' he told me, 'we've kicked the ball through the kitchen window. We didn't mean it, honestly! What will Dad say?' This was the first I knew of it as I was unable to hear the glass shattering. 'Don't worry,' I assured him, 'it was an accident. I'll pray that Dad won't blow a fuse.' Ewan thanked me and went back out to play. Dave's response when he saw what had happened brought a smile to his son's face. 'Don't worry,' his dad told him. 'We'll get a new pane of glass tomorrow.' 'Mum,' Ewan said, having raced to my side, 'your prayer worked!' That was a lesson we were all learning.

What if?

It would be dishonest to suggest that remorse never ate at us, and it was brought on by brooding on little things. One Christmas Ruth had asked for a baby doll. Having been given one the previous year, she called her Jane, we thought a different gift would be more appropriate, though all she really wanted was a sister for Jane. Why did we deny a second doll that would have been equally loved, or the rabbit Ruth longed for? Not getting what she wanted must have hurt her, and now it hurt me if I let myself dwell on it. Had Ruth lived I am sure these things would not even have been remembered. Thankfully, when such thoughts come to mind, I can usually discern that Satan is their source. Scripture warns us to, 'Be self-controlled and alert. Your enemy the devil prowls around like a roaring lion looking for someone to devour' (1 Peter 5:8). If we allow the enemy to keep picking at these scars they will fester. But thankfully God can, and does, heal the pain of such recollections so that they do not remain dark patches that blight our happy memories.

No one who has not gone through it totally understands the emptiness experienced on losing a child. But God does. One day I found myself telling the Lord that he had given me more than I could cope with. Suddenly I felt the sensation of a sharp sword piercing my heart, and remembered the Lord Jesus' words from the cross, 'My God, my God, why have you forsaken me?' (Mark 15:34). Yes, God understood. He had not only lost, he had given his own dear Son to die on the cross for me. God understood exactly what we were going through, even the timing of it was in his hands.

Mission partner, faithful friend
Although at times it can be hard to understand God's dealings with us, I believe that he does all things right and that he times everything perfectly. Shortly after Ewan was born in 1979, my minister asked if I would correspond with our church's missionary partner in Malawi, Elsabe Irvine. My immediate reaction was, 'Oh

no, lots of people would be far more able to do that than me.' But my 'no' was not accepted. After corresponding for years, Elsabe came to live with us for two weeks while she was home on furlough. One evening I confided in her that, although I believed in God and the resurrection of his Son Jesus Christ, for two or three reasons I did not think I was a Christian. The conversation that followed was used by the Lord to bring me into a real and saving relationship with him.

My life began to change as I surrendered to my Lord. Attitudes were challenged, and prayer became deeper and more meaningful. God had become real in his presence, not just a celestial Being sitting on his heavenly throne looking earthwards. And I discovered that God's Word, the Bible, could be savoured, not just read. The following year I became totally deaf, and two years later Ruth's illness was diagnosed. With hindsight I see that was exactly as God had planned. He knew when he was to take Ruth home, and he prepared the way for me by holding me close to himself. He also prepared the way for Ruth. One evening after our second visit to Yorkhill, Ruth said to me, 'Mum, you've always said I've been very brave. I know now that it's not me who's being brave, it's Jesus inside me.' It was one of the greatest privileges of my life, that the Saviour used me to bring Ruth to himself, as he had used Elsabe to bring me.

Fix your eyes on Jesus

All through my Christian life I have known that God is a God of his word. And following Ruth's death, I discovered that scriptural truth in a deeper and more urgent way. 'God is faithful; he will not let you be tempted (tested) beyond what you can bear. But when you are tempted (tested), he will also provide a way out so that you can stand up under it' (1 Corinthians 10:13). One day when I was praying, it came to me that when I thought of her I should focus on the risen Ruth. I worship a risen Saviour, my daughter is now with him in glory, and I should focus, not on the memory of a dead daughter, but on the promise of one who is risen. What a promise! What a Saviour!

When visiting a friend in her home, she pointed me to a verse in *A Child Loaned* which read, 'I'll lend you for a little while a child of mine, he said.' The words leapt out at me. I think I had forgotten that Ruth was first and foremost God's child. What a thing to forget. Thankfully the Lord reminded me of this in a very loving, but firm way. When praying a few days later God told me 'to give and not to count the cost', thus refusing to focus on my earthly loss, and to focus only on him and in the knowledge that our daughter was safe in his care.

Nine months after Ruth died, just before Christmas, I experienced whiplash after a car bumped into the back of ours at a pedestrian crossing. This resulted in me having to wear a thick surgical collar for three months. Not for a second do I think God caused the accident, but he certainly did use it. When Christmas Day came, the collar and my restricted movement certainly occupied part of our thoughts, and diverted the three of us just a little bit from focusing on it being our first Christmas without Ruth.

A very emotional time hit me a year later, just before Christmas 1988, when I found myself in tears on many occasions. This was very upsetting for Ewan, who was nine years old. He would say, 'Mummy, please stop crying,' and, try though I did, I could not. Some close friends asked if perhaps I had not shed enough tears during the first few months following Ruth's death. But if I needed to cry then, I cried, and never consciously bottled up any tearful emotions. I know I got through that time in God's strength, but I'm only human, and God understood my tears.

It is now fourteen years since Ruth died. She has been longer in heaven than she was on earth. Facing what would have been birthdays, especially significant ones like her eighteenth and twenty-first, has been hard, as has 4th March, the day Ruth died. The Lord alone carries us through these days. It has been my experience that God's love, as well as being deeply compassionate and caring, can be described as 'an energy rather than an emotion' (Agnes Sanford in *Sealed Orders*). It surrounds and enfolds us, it wells up within us, it carries and uplifts us. It meets us exactly where our need is and provides the strength to endure, and peace and victory in the doing of it. Without our Lord's love I would crumble and fall, perhaps even rebel.

Ruth's Yorkhill Fund

Looking back over our experiences, Dave and I know that good has come out of the suffering. On her visits to Yorkhill Hospital, before entering her single room where she had to remain for her five days of treatment, Ruth saw many sick children, mainly babies and toddlers. She was so keen to do something to help them that, after being given the all clear, she planned to have a coffee morning in our church hall at which she hoped to raise around £200 to give to her professor to buy something that would be of help. Our daughter wrote in a notebook those who were to be invited to help, and what she wanted them to do. Sadly Ruth died two weeks before the date, but her coffee morning went ahead raising, not the hoped for £200, but £1,200. It was a fine tribute to a fine girl.

Not long thereafter, 'Ruth's Yorkhill Fund'

was established. From that coffee morning until the Fund closed ten years later, just over £65,000 was raised. Research into children's cancers was to be undertaken at Yorkhill Hospital, but the funding for it was just an annual grant. Ruth's Fund helped to provide much-needed research equipment. One event we found particularly touching was a fashion show which Ruth's classmates put on when they reached their final school year. It raised just over £1,252. But every fund-raising event counted, however small. Every penny was needed for research.

Closing the fund was not easy as our hearts had been so fully in it during its years of existence. The Lord led me in the direction of closure, and after a few months of hesitancy I obeyed his will and received his peace. God's Word says, 'There is a time for everything, and a season for every activity under heaven' (Ecclesiastes 3:1). As Christians, we must allow the Lord to be the time setter. He knows best. Ruth's professor was overwhelmed with the Fund's time span, and the research equipment it was able to provide. Thankfully other parents who have lost children also donate to this worthy cause.

I felt led to write a little book, *One Small Life – Ruth*, two years after our daughter died. Each of the 2,400 books printed was sold. The thought never entered my mind that I would receive any letters following publication, but the response was quite overwhelming. It was very humbling to know that the account of Ruth's short life was used to help readers in a variety of ways. We could never have guessed that would happen.

The jigsaw of Ruth's life and her Yorkhill Fund has been put together and is now complete. The jigsaw of all our lives has pieces already in place, and others the Lord will slot in at his chosen time. God's grace turned my spiritual darkness into light, and his love and comfort helped dispel the darkness of Ruth's death. I would never pretend for a moment that tears are not still shed, but fourteen years on, when a tear suddenly trickles down my cheek, often when least expected, God understands. Jesus knows I am human and it comforts me to remember that my human Lord Jesus wept when his close friend Lazarus died. Although the passing of time can soothe the pain of losing a dearly loved one, the Lord alone can heal it.

2

KEITH WESTON

Nobody would deny that growing old can have its problems. It all depends on how we view the process. Down the years there have been many depressing exponents of a pessimistic frame of mind, from Hippocrates in the fifth century BC who likened the ages of man to the four seasons, and old age was winter of course; to Disraeli who wrote: 'Youth is a blunder; manhood a struggle; old age a regret.' They seem to agree that 'good health is only the slowest possible rate at which one can die'!

As I have watched the years go past, it has encouraged me that while Scripture is honest about growing old, it is never pessimistic. 'The length of our days is seventy years – or eighty if we have the strength. Yet their span is but trouble and sorrow; for they quickly pass and we fly away' (Psalm 90:10). But I am assured that, as a Christian, I am secure in the gracious hand of God. 'Your eyes saw my unformed body. All the days ordained for me were written in your book before one of them came to be' (Psalm 139:16). I believe, therefore, that we who are

God's people can grow old grace-fully, i.e. full of the knowledge of the grace of God at work in our lives, and knowing that he knows the way we take. Our Lord simply asks us, with his teaching help, to 'number our days that we may gain a heart of wisdom' (Psalm 90:12). That assures me that he knows how long I have left here on earth, down to the very last day, and that he expects me to live what is left of my time responsibly.

The big question

In common with most other older people, I've become very aware of the passage of time. I love the words on the clock at Chester Cathedral:

> When as a child I laughed and wept, time crept.
> When as a youth I waxed more bold, time
> strolled.
> When I became a full-grown man, time ran.
> When older still I grew, time flew.
> Soon I shall find, in passing on, time gone ...

The inscription finishes with the prayer:

> O Christ! Wilt thou have saved me then?

I thank God that as a believer my answer is, 'Yes,' and that my life, including whatever is left of it, is preparation for glory, that great hope set before every child of God.

But I am not just sitting around thinking about the past and waiting for heaven. God would have me use each day to the full in his glad service. Looking back may harbour regrets; that's why it is so important to live so that we can say at the end with the Apostle Paul, 'I have fought the good fight, I have finished the race, I have kept the faith' (2 Timothy 4:7).

Meeting Jesus

I had the great privilege of being born to Christian parents, the youngest of three boys. But it was at the age of eleven, at a wartime Christian Harvest Camp, that I realised for the first time what Jesus had done for me on the cross, and I dedicated my life to him as best I knew how. The words of Isaiah 53:5-6 became crystal clear to me. 'He was wounded for our transgressions. He was bruised for our iniquities: the chastisement of our peace was upon him; and with his stripes we are healed. All we like sheep have gone astray; we have turned every one to his own way; and the Lord hath laid on him the iniquity of us all.' (Those were the days of the Authorised Version!)

I did not then know where God might lead me, but I heard the call to ordination years later, while serving in the army through four challenging years in Italy and Palestine. Palestine planted in my heart a love for Jews and Arabs, and I felt I was being called to do missionary work there. But at the end of my Cambridge years, when I had studied with that call in mind, I had the bewildering experience of being turned down by the mission with which I had hoped to serve. But the mission was right; God had other plans, and via ordination and involvement with the Keswick Convention all over the world, I have been given opportunities which might be the envy of many in full-time service overseas.

Did my godly Edinburgh granny have something to do with this? When I was twelve, I was rushed to hospital from a cricket match at school for what appeared to be a straightforward appendix operation. In fact, my life hung in the balance during surgery, which took three hours to perform. I was seven weeks confined to bed. When I was past the worst, Granny wrote to me and said in her forthright way that God had preserved my life and given me more years to spend for him, adding that she believed that there must be some particular work that God wanted me to do. She also enclosed a whole pound note – a lot of money then. But, to my utter disappointment, she said I was to give it to a missionary society as a thank-offering! Rather cross with her, I did what she said – and my father gave me another one! Now, at the age of seventy-four and looking back, I see that these years have often been punctuated by experiences which were difficult at the time, but which led me in the way God had planned ahead for me, 'good works which God prepared in advance for us to do' (Ephesians 2:10).

Calm in the storm
More recently I was again brought near to death. A run of heart attacks and a cardiac arrest asked all the right questions: Where is God in this? Will I still be here in the morning? How should I balance my eager Christian hope of glory with thoughts of how much there is still to do? When all wired up to the usual machinery and festooned with drips, there was plenty of room for fear and anxiety; yet I can honestly say that while my dear wife suffered terrible anxieties, I spent most of the time in peace. My only worry was that I found it hard to pray, though I am sure that God was there beside me all the time. The hospital chaplain said, 'We'll do the praying; you just get better!' But what was such a lifeline was remembering and repeating to myself over and over again the Scripture passages that had been so special to me in past years. Verses like, 'I consider that our present sufferings are not worth comparing with the glory that will be revealed in us' (Romans 8:18) came often to my mind.

My one regret was that I found it hard to remember all I wanted to remember, and it was so helpful to have Scripture read to me during those days. As an Anglican, I must add that some of the old Prayer Book became even more precious. My days finished with, 'Lighten our darkness, we beseech Thee, O Lord, and by Thy great mercy defend us from all perils and dangers of this night.' And my mornings began, 'O Lord our heavenly Father, Almighty and everlasting God, who hast safely brought us to the beginning of this day...' Those words, which alongside Scripture have run in my spiritual bloodstream since childhood days, became even more precious. And I thank God that once again he has thought fit to give me more time, and to rejoice in the privilege and opportunities of preaching in the country churches near where we live, where clergy and ministers are thin on the ground, and where humble ministry is so appreciated. But how I long for the energy I once had!

Not too old to reach out

Having become one of the elderly, and having undergone such a health scare, has made me realise more than ever before the need for the church to minister to older people. We place much emphasis on 'the youth' and employ youth leaders at great expense, but the elderly are sometimes seen (it would appear) as an embarrassment, and even something of a nuisance, always 'resistant to change'. Yet there is a great evangelistic opportunity there, because we who are elderly realise much more than younger folk that our days are numbered and we will soon be gone. For the non-Christian, thoughts arise about death and what lies beyond the grave. But for the Christian, of course, 'to be with Christ which is better by far' (Philippians 1:23) is the assured hope for which we long. What is so wonderful to us must surely be our aim to share with those who have no hope and who are 'without God in this world' (Ephesians 2:12). And it is good to remind ourselves that we have a unique opportunity to reach out to our ageing contemporaries, who are as aware as we are of the passing of the years.

Body: the problem?

While growing old is part and parcel of life, it requires a lot of godly acceptance on our part. I have not found it easy to avoid talking about my problems at the drop of a hat. We can be such miseries, and there are many better things to talk about. As a Christian I have to remind myself to think positively, to think from Paul's perspective: 'We do not lose heart. Though outwardly we are wasting away, yet inwardly we are being renewed day by day. For our light and momentary troubles are achieving for us an eternal glory that far outweighs them all. So we fix our eyes not on what is seen, but on what is

35

unseen. For what is seen is temporary, but what is unseen is eternal' (2 Corinthians 4:16-18). It can be difficult to keep that perspective. We can be only too aware of the body 'wasting away', and we wish that the continual inward renewing could be just as obvious.

Mind: the puzzle?
Our minds are also affected by increasing age. It is my experience that as we get older we tend to become more susceptible to the strains and stresses of life, with decreasing resources of the resilience that once helped us cope. They play upon our minds, especially if circumstances allow us too much time to think. I tend to sleep very lightly, and my brain sometimes loves to chew over many things in the small hours of the night, and to keep me awake as it does it. I have had to learn to look to Jesus, to focus upon him and to let his peace take over.

Change is a problem with many of us older people, and I admit that there are aspects of it which I have found particularly difficult, especially as it touches church life and worship. I fully understand that for the vast majority of non-church people, what is precious to us is utterly irrelevant to them, and we simply have to try to reach out to them in meaningful ways. As a pastor, I know how difficult this can be, and have myself from time to time been criticised for introducing into worship things unfamiliar to old folk. So I am not against change: but it matters very much what is changed and how changes are made. It sometimes feels as though we older people are being sidelined and ostracised, robbed of so many of the things which have been precious to us for decades. What has become of the best of the old hymns – especially when replaced by repetitive songs with little content (though many new hymns and songs are superb). What too has become of reverence? Why is noise thought to be so essential? Silence is no longer golden to the modern age. I have often thought of what is said in Deuteronomy 19:14, though admittedly taken out of context, 'You shall not remove your neighbour's landmark, set up by your predecessors.' Sometimes it feels as though the landmarks of our faith have been bulldozed.

Acceptance can be one of the surest marks of a grace-full old age. We need to cultivate the grace to let God take the heavy end of our worries and anxieties and fears. I was never very good at remembering names. Now I am hopeless. And I'm not alone. Memory loss seems to be one of the first things many of us experience, and we may have to take practical steps to contain it. I find it harder to avoid being oversensitive, easily hurt or given to making judgments on others who seem critical or unjust, and often based on misunderstanding. And those of us who have been in leadership roles sometimes find it hard to be led rather than taking the lead. There is real potential for cantankerousness and self-importance. And how I and others like me must pray that our old age will be marked by humility, even when we have good grounds for holding our own opinions.

Spirit: the lifeline!
There are some spiritual lessons that ageing is teaching me, and I am sure that many of my contemporaries are finding the same. They concern our spiritual life. It is sobering to find in Scripture that some of the greatest saints suffered spectacular failures in their later years. Noah, Gideon, even David cut a sad figure in old age. The Bible gives us a warning: 'So, if you think you are standing firm, be careful that you don't fall' (1 Corinthians 10:12). But there are other elderly saints who are a great example to us. Anna, 'very old' and a widow, never left the temple, a woman of prayer indeed. And the magnificent Caleb, eighty-five-years-old when he asked Joshua to give him one of the toughest parts of the Promised Land to possess!

It is clear that Scripture sees that the devotional life of elderly folk is as vital to their spiritual life as ever it was. 'God gives strength to the weary and increases the power of the weak.

For even youths grow tired and are weary, and young men stumble and fall; but those who hope in the LORD (The Revised Standard Version says 'wait on the LORD') will renew their strength' (Isaiah 40:29-31). But there are some nasty temptations to make us stumble and fall. Doubt can be a terrible disease, tormenting the mind even of those with an active Christian life of service behind them. Liberal and radical theology don't help, especially as radio and television pelts us with those supposedly newsworthy people who seem to take pleasure in casting doubt on, even denying, the great truths of our faith. Once we could think it out and cope with it, but now we find our resistance weakened and the foundation of our assurance (though not of our salvation) can be seriously undermined.

And guilt can be another terrible disease. Looking back over the past we may wonder if we truly can be forgiven. The devil is the accuser of our souls, and he is not kind to old folk. We must hold on to God's gracious promises and not listen to Satan's insinuations. 'If we confess our sins God is faithful and just and will forgive us our sins and cleanse us from ALL unrighteousness' (1 John 1:9). When our sins leap up and accuse us, God's promise is 'I will remember their sins no more' (Jeremiah 31:34). Guilt can be associated with regrets, many of them understandable, as none of us have lived our past years or used our potential to the full in pleasing God. But some regrets go bad on us, especially in bereavement when we are no longer able to put right something that was long overdue. As I age, and as more of those I know pass away, that is something I have to keep at the forefront of my thinking. It has been said that we should keep short accounts with God, but it seems to me that we should do the same with our fellow men.

While old age robs us of our faculties to some degree or another, and while it throws up spiritual assaults of its own, we must never allow it to rob us of a close walk with God. It challenges me when I read in Scripture of those who allowed that to happen, and it heartens me when I read of those who did not.

Bonus time blessings

The passage of years has its compensations, and they far outweigh the difficulties. My wife and I have been spared to each other, and we thank God from the bottom of our hearts for that. And over the last few years we have been able to cultivate the enjoyment of each other's company and do things together. We've fallen in love all over again. And we have been able to give unhurried time to reading the Bible and praying together.

The best is yet to be

For the believer, however hard life may become, one bright factor shines through it all. This is the wonder of the hope set before us in Christ, and what a prospect that is as we approach death. Hebrews speaks of 'full assurance of hope' (6:11, RSV) because 'we have this hope as an anchor for the soul, firm and secure' (6:19). It is in this hope that we have been saved (Romans 8:24), and its full measure is beautifully expressed in Paul's quotation of the Old Testament in 1 Corinthians 2:9: 'No eye has seen, no ear has heard, no mind has conceived what God has prepared for those who love him.' So, as we often affirm – and how wonderfully true it is – death is not the end but a glorious new beginning. Heaven is the wonderful prospect for the believer, where 'the dwelling place of God is with man,... and God himself will be with them and be their God. He will wipe away every tear from their eyes. There will be no more death or mourning or crying or pain, for the old order of things has passed away' (Revelation 21:3-4).

As a pastor I have often read these words to seriously ill or bereaved members of my congregation, and I bear testimony to the comfort and peace – even eager anticipation – that this hope brought me personally when lying in hospital. Add to this doctrine of the Christian's hope in Christ the absolutely thrilling doctrine of his resurrection, and our breath is taken away! Paul writes that the Saviour 'will transform our lowly bodies so that they will be like his glorious body' (Philippians 3:21), a truth which he expounds at thrilling length in 1 Corinthians 15.

Jesus, we are told, 'for the joy set before him, endured the cross' (Hebrews 12:2). Surely, for the joy set before us, we too can by grace endure the comparably trivial effects of what life brings to us in our later years. We are to 'run with perseverance the race marked out for us' (especially the last lap!). Let us fix our eyes on Jesus, the author and perfector of our faith' (Hebrews 12:1-2). We, I, must grow old gracefully.

3

BERTIE AND PAT JOHNSTON

Bertie begins the story

One winter's day in Manchester, with no money in my pockets, one of my shoes leaking and feeling hungry and cold, I took my watch off my wrist and looked at it. That watch was a treasured gift, but I pawned it. How did a respectable young man from County Fermanagh come to be pawning his watch in Manchester? That is a sad story.

I was the youngest boy in a family of three boys and two girls, brought up on a farm near Derrygonnelly. My mother, a religious woman, sent us to the local Methodist Church Sunday School. Dad, who farmed and had a milk haulier's business, was fond of drinking and gambling. Having left school at fourteen to help on the farm, I took over the haulier's business just as soon as I passed my driving test. But, despite so much going for me, I threw restraint to the wind and drank and smoked and gambled. By the time I was twenty-one, between my father and myself, we had run the business to ruin. So bad did things become that we sold out and I, full of anger and bitterness towards my father, left home in January 1967, left Ulster, and left my common sense behind.

Pat shares her background
Born and bred in a strict Roman Catholic home and educated by the Sisters of Mercy, I imbibed the teachings of the Roman Catholic Church and was a devout young person in my teens. By my early twenties I was beginning to ask awkward questions, questions for which I could not get answers. Although I continued to attend mass and confession and other church meetings, things by then were different. I was no longer a devout Catholic, and I had lost my desire for prayer.

Bertie
For thirteen months I battled with the pull of home, the lure of the sinful city and the agony of a guilty conscience. Pride and stubbornness held me back, but eventually I got the boat over the Irish Sea, in rags, penniless, hungry, and with no friends. And there was no welcome at the door of my home, for both my father and mother were in hospital. After a time of wondering what to do, I decided I would stay at home and look after them. At least that gave me a roof over my head and people who cared. For a while I didn't go out for fear of meeting acquaintances who would ask awkward questions about my time in England,

but after some months I swallowed my pride and took up my old life where I had left it off.

It was the following year, 1969, that I met Pat in our local supermarket. I knew she was from a Roman Catholic home, but got into conversation with her all the same, and even asked her out for a date. Our courtship was marked by many family quarrels on both sides. Although that hurt us both, it did not break our relationship.

Pat

Bertie came to mass with me once, but when he was there he saw a very drunk man praying with rosary beads and that upset him badly. As he pushed his way to the door of the chapel at the end of the service, Bertie told me that he would never be in a place like that again. From the chapel we went to a hotel for a drink. Some time later, I asked Bertie to take me to a Protestant church. He didn't want to because he never went himself, but I won that argument and we went to look for one.

Bertie

I didn't know where to find a church, but we passed one on the main street that was advertising the Irish Evangelistic Band Annual Convention. After a furtive glance at the hotel across the road from the church to make sure nobody we knew could see us, we went in. The preacher was Rev. Sidney Martin, and what he said spoke right to Pat's heart. She wouldn't even go for a drink afterwards! I returned home and spent a sleepless night.

Pat

I went to church that evening out of curiosity, and Bertie accompanied me to keep me happy. The preacher spoke about a certain Roman Catholic who had felt just as I did, and he told how she had got an answer to her problems by asking God, in the name of Jesus Christ, to forgive all her sin. I sat up and listened as I'd never done before. I could feel God's presence in the service, and I knew the Holy Spirit was talking right to me. It all became clear – I was a sinner, and I had to come in true repentance and simple faith to Christ and ask him to come into my heart. I could not hold myself back. I grasped the offer eagerly and was born again.

Bertie

Among the many things that spun round in my mind in the dark hours of that night was the memory of an uncle who had often spoken to me about his 'precious Saviour'. Even though it was the middle of the night, I got up, found his name in the phone book, and dialled his number. 'I'll be right round in the morning,' he assured me, when I told him why I had phoned. The following morning my uncle showed me clearly from the Scriptures that I was a sinner and that Christ died for me. Before we parted that day, I was born again. Immediately the devil tempted me with thoughts of what Pat would think. That evening I realised that Pat had also had an encounter with the Lord and had trusted him as Saviour. A short while later we were married.

In October 1970, I joined the Royal Ulster Constabulary, serving in one of County Armagh's larger towns. That was at the beginning of troubled times in Northern Ireland. Within two years I was to find myself in the thick of it. One autumn Sunday afternoon in 1972, I was on beat duty with a colleague when we were spotted by terrorists who went for guns then came back to shoot us. While they were away the rain came on. As we passed a house, a gentleman at the door invited us to step in out of the rain. He was quite unknown to us, but we accepted his kind offer. As we were sheltering, the gunmen drove past in search of us. When they didn't find us, they turned the corner of the street and caught sight of some off duty soldiers, one of whom they gunned down. That young man was the first soldier in County Armagh to be killed by terrorists in the Troubles. My colleague and I attended the incident, unaware that the soldier had died instead of us. It was only later, when being questioned regarding another matter, that the terrorists divulged this information. And during their trial they gave a graphic description of the events of that day and I discovered how the Lord had spared us. My heart ached for the family of that young soldier. His murder brought home to me in a most profound way what it meant for the Lord to die in my stead at Calvary. My colleague was murdered by terrorists four years later.

After three and a half years I was promoted to sergeant and transferred to the city of Londonderry. I served there with the CID and the Regional Crime Squad, and from then until I left my job I was dealing with terrorism. In each of my first eight weeks in Londonderry, someone was murdered on the west bank of the Foyle River. So bad was the situation, that when we left home in the morning we really didn't know if we'd ever be back again. One day there would be a room with fifteen detectives, the following day there would be an aching silence and an empty desk.

Pat

Bertie and I were blessed with two daughters. Claire was born in 1972 and her little sister, Karen, came nearly three years later. We became very involved in the work and witness of our church, although my husband's shift patterns made that difficult for him. I could not but be aware of the dangers his job involved, but I had to learn to hand him over to the Lord's safekeeping as he left our home each day. God promises that he will always be with his people, and I proved the truth of that promise over and over again at that time.

Bertie

One Sunday in 1978, three men in a hijacked car went three times to our church looking for me, turning up at the 11 am Breaking of Bread, the 3 pm Sunday School and the 7.30 pm Gospel service. They knew about Pat and the girls, they knew what my normal movements were, they had my car registration number, they knew where I lived, and they were out to get me. Had it been a normal Sunday I would have been shot, and who knows what might have happened to my family. However, that week a colleague offered to lend us his caravan for the weekend. It was along the coast at Portrush. Having made a last-minute decision to take the Sunday off, we spent a relaxing few days in the caravan, unaware that by guiding us there the Lord had saved our lives. Two weeks later, terrorists were arrested for the murder of another policeman and, while being questioned, they told of their efforts to kill me. Two of these men were released after questioning which meant that we had to move, and quickly.

Pat

We hadn't long purchased a lovely bungalow a few miles out of Londonderry when that incident happened. I was obviously perturbed when Bertie told me the news, and that we were under police guard and had to move immediately. We got down to pray, side by side by our bed, with our Bible in front of us. As we committed the situation to the Lord, the Bible slipped off the bed and opened at Psalm 21. Both of us looked down, and God led our eyes to verse 11. 'For they intended evil against thee: they imagined a mischievous device, which they are not able to perform.' Peace filled our hearts. Bertie felt he could have stayed on in Londonderry on the basis of that verse, but the RUC moved us, and transferred him to the same kind of work in Armagh.

As the girls grew older, they became more aware of the Troubles, and of their daddy's job. Inevitably they also became aware of the dangerous situations he found himself in from time to time. We prayed for them and we prayed with them. Despite it all, it was almost inconceivable to me that my husband could do any other job. He loved his work. He had been in the RUC ten years, and was heading for promotion once again.

Bertie

In 1980, I went to Hendon in England, to do a course at the Police Training Centre there. This was with a view to further promotion. I loved every minute of the course and really looked forward to putting into practice what I learned. Job-wise I had everything going for me. And Pat, although it could not have been easy for her, understood my passion for the police and supported me as I climbed the career ladder. In a way I felt that what I was doing was for her and the girls, and for all the other ordinary families in the Province who were threatened by the Troubles.

I had also seen thrilling blessings in the course of my duties. Some terrorists I met through my work became Christians. One, who is now an elder in his church, was born again as a result of reading my testimony in his prison cell. And there was the opportunity to talk to my colleagues too. We regularly attended post-mortems where we saw some truly terrible things. That brought us face-to-face with the brevity of life and the finality of death, and it opened up many opportunities to talk of the only One in whom there is hope for eternity.

Very soon after returning from Hendon, I took an hour off work one quiet Sunday and went to the local Baptist church. The pastor preached on Mark 11:1-11. In that passage, Jesus and the disciples arrive at Bethphage and Bethany on the outskirts of Jerusalem. The Lord sent two of his friends into the village, telling them that they would find a colt tied up there, one that had never been ridden, and that they were to bring it back to him. This they did, and the Lord sat on the unbroken colt and on it entered the city of Jerusalem amid a cheering crowd, the same crowd that would demand his crucifixion just a few days later. The preacher pointed out that as long as the colt was tied up, it was of no use to the Lord. It had to be loosed to be of use. God spoke to me through that sermon, showing me that my lovely home, security, material things and promotion were tying me down. As the service came to an end, I asked God through my tears, to show me unmistakably if he wanted me out of the RUC, but even then I knew in my heart of hearts that I had to resign. Stubbornly I waited for further confirmation of what I knew to be right. It came some months later. But what was I to do? I hadn't preached very much, I had no congregation to minister to, and no mission to support me. But I knew, without a shadow of doubt, that I had to leave the RUC and engage in some kind of full-time ministry.

Pat
My husband was quite sure the Lord was leading him, and we had no choice but obey. Even the

girls understood that. By the time we sold the house and sorted out all our financial affairs we had £100 we could call our own. Sometimes over the months that followed, we had few resources. But the Lord always provided for us, and we never went without. His tender care for us has strengthened my faith over the years. He took Bertie from being a policeman to being a preacher, giving him a ministry that eventually extended from Armagh to the whole of the United Kingdom and beyond.

Bertie introduces the Lifeboat Mission
I started off as a travelling missionary, taking meetings here, there and everywhere. Having worked in a sectarian situation, where people carried arms and used them against those on the other side of the religious divide, I was led by the Lord to preach the gospel message, the good news that people of differing backgrounds can live together, if their life together is in Christ. Not long into my ministry I secured a portable hall which was moved from place to place as my ministry took me.

While driving through the Moy district one evening in 1987, I was deeply exercised in heart over the spiritual condition of that town and its surrounding area. Many places of worship were closed on Lord's Day evenings and most of the public houses were open. Over the following months four friends and I made that a matter of earnest prayer. In the spring of 1988, a site became available, the portable hall was set up, and the work in Moy began with fifty people in attendance on the first night. Since then many souls have been saved, and scores of people have sought baptism. By June the following year, the hall which seated one hundred was too small for those who met together and the Lord wonderfully provided an extension.

It was in the autumn of 1990 that we again found ourselves short of accommodation, and by then we were holding a morning Breaking of Bread service as well as our evening Gospel meeting. Then the Lord brought about a remarkable happening. Adjacent to the hall there was a bungalow with several outbuildings, including a hen house full of 5,000 hens. The owner intimated his intention of selling, and offered us the first option on the property. God spoke to my fellow elder through Luke 5:4 in the Authorised Version of the Bible, 'Launch out into the deep, and let down your nets for a draught.' And he directed me through an Old Testament passage: 'For the land, whither thou goest in to possess it, is not as the land of Egypt, from whence ye came out, where thou sowedst thy seed, and wateredst it with thy foot, as a garden of herbs: But the land, whither ye go to possess it, is a land of hills and valleys, and drinketh water of the rain of heaven' (Deuteronomy 11:10-11, AV). That for me was amazing confirmation that we should go ahead with buying the property, as the piece of land in question had within its boundaries a hill, a valley and a river. Work on the former hen house transformed it, and in January 1993 the Lifeboat Mission was opened and dedicated to the service of the Lord. Since then it has been much used as a place of worship. And for many people it is the place where they came to know the Saviour.

As a member of the Royal Ulster Constabulary I fought against the evils of terrorism, and in the course of duty was faced with the great issues of life and death on a daily basis. In a way my ministry is a continuation of the same thing. I am still engaged in a life and death battle as I preach the warning of eternal damnation and the glorious invitation to eternal life. I believe I was saved to serve, first in the RUC then through the inestimable privilege of the gospel ministry.

4

HOPE SCOTT

I was a war time baby, the First World War. Mother was from the north west coast of Wales and father from a mining valley, but work had taken them to the Cardiff area before I came along. When I was in my teens I went to live with my granny in a little mining village. It was not unusual for girls to do that in those days.

After leaving school I found work in a local grocery shop. Groceries sold at one end of the shop and butcher meat at the other. The store behind the shop was full of sacks of flour, oats, lentils, peas, barley, all the things that are bought in neat polythene packets today. Then shop assistants weighed and measured everything out of two hundredweight sacks. There was a whole gantry of cheeses to be skinned and hams to be cut. Butter came in huge blocks from which we cut the required amount before pressing it into shape with wooden butter pats. Upstairs was full of cattle feed, and behind the shop was where the cattle were slaughtered. I dread to think what a modern day environmental health officer would have thought of it! Our hours were long. Shops opening late is nothing new. We opened at 8 am and closed at 8 pm, 9 pm on Saturdays.

Jesus, my friend

The man I worked for also had the butcher's shop next door, and it was there that Tom Wilson worked. Tom was a tall and handsome young man. He, like me, was brought up to attend the church in the village. I can't remember a time when I didn't believe in the Lord Jesus, and by the time I had grown up my faith was living and real. Jesus was not just someone I heard about in sermons on Sundays, he was my friend every day of the week. In those days our church was well attended and the worship was led by a choir of which I was a member. In our tradition we sing metrical psalms, the book of Psalms in verse form, and as a young woman my heart just filled when we sang such great psalms of praise as this:

> Now blessed be the Lord our God,
> the God of Israel,
> For he alone doth wondrous works,
> in glory that excel.
> And blessed be his glorious name
> to all eternity:
> The whole earth let his glory fill.
> Amen, so let it be.
> (Psalm 72:18-19, Scottish metrical version)

We sang in parts, and we raised the roof. Perhaps that's why it is in such a poor state today!

Tom, whom I married, was the eldest of quite a big family, all of whom lived in the village. His father kept poor health and died young. Tom's grandfather had been the same, but I never knew him. It seemed that my father-in-law suffered from what was then called premature ageing. It was sad to watch him waste away and die. But life went on, and Tom and I had hard but happy years in front of us. It was hard for everyone then. There was little money for necessities, and none to spare, but we were content, and we felt blessed beyond measure when our first son, Evan, was born. Two years later he was big brother to Hew, and the following year Ian came along. Our joy, and our family, was complete. The boys had a happy childhood, with all the freedom that came from living in a small, tight-knit community. Some people who move into a village find it hard to cope with everyone knowing what everyone else is doing. It can be irritating, especially if they get it wrong. But most of the time, it gives a real sense of security, and it was in that kind of secure community that our boys were brought up.

A puzzling problem
But a cloud came over the horizon. Tom started to stagger from time to time; nothing dramatic,

but it was worrying. He could misjudge a step or stumble over nothing. We thought it would pass. Probably some folk in the village thought he was taking a drink too many. I knew that whatever the problem was, it was not drink. And it did not pass. Over time his lack of balance grew more noticeable and people would ask if Tom was all right. There were dark comments made about his father's illness. Tests were done, but no name could be put to his problem.

Evan, Hew and Ian were in their teens when Tom's condition became so bad that he had to give up work. By then his walking was hazardous and his speech was affected too. It was as though everything apart from his mind was slowing down. Sunday by Sunday I stood in church, singing the psalms with all my heart. David, who wrote most of the psalms, knew what problems were and he wrote from the depths of his own experience. I could identify with the words as I sang them, especially, as I saw Tom losing ground, with the words of Psalm 107:

> They reel and stagger like one drunk,
> at their wit's end they be:
> Then they to God in trouble cry,
> who them from straits sets free.
>
> The storm is chang'd into a calm,
> at his command and will;
> So that the waves, which rag'd before
> now quiet are and still.

> Then they are glad, because at rest
> and quiet now they be;
> So to the haven he them brings
> which they desir'd to see.
>
> (Psalm 107:27-30, Scottish metrical version)

In the storms that arose in our souls, as Tom's ability to walk, to work and to talk all deteriorated, our haven was Christ. He gave us a supportive family and the very best of friends, but, in the end of the day, only he knew what we were going through. Only he knew our fears for the future and the hopes that we would never see fulfilled.

The boys were wonderful. They carried their dad up and down stairs, lifted him into his wheelchair and took him for walks along the main street where he could see everyone coming and going, and catch up on the local news. And I needed them to help, because I had to work all the hours I could to earn enough for us to live on. It is never easy to have illness or disability in a family, but I am glad that those who go through that today have state benefits to provide for them when they can't earn for themselves.

Fears for the future

By the time Tom died, we were seeing the early symptoms of the same problem in other members of his family. Everyone tried to avoid voicing the conclusions that we were all coming to, that

61

there was a problem in the family that, God forbid, might be passed on to our children. For Tom's sisters, like us, had families of their own. When my husband passed away I discovered the reality of the psalm that had so often comforted me over the years.

> Yea, though I walk in death's dark vale,
> yet will I fear none ill;
> For thou art with me; and thy rod
> and staff me comfort still.
> (Psalm 23:4, Scottish metrical version)

Tom was taken away, but Jesus was faithful. He remained my constant companion, even in the dark days when I couldn't feel him there.

Our sons grew to be fine young men and before many years had passed they were married. I felt proud but lonely at their weddings. How I longed that Tom could have been standing beside me. And I felt that even more so when the grandchildren started to come along. But what pleasure they gave me. There is nothing like grandchildren to make you feel young again, even when the years are catching up on you! They lived near enough for me to see them often, to watch their first steps and hear their first words; to see them all dressed in their new school clothes, to watch their wobbly teeth and to bathe their skinned knees. Being a granny suited me just fine.

The hard facts

But it was not only the grandchildren that kept me busy. Having seen Tom waste away I decided, along with some others in the village, to raise funds to research his family's strange condition. We ran all sorts of events and raised thousands of pounds. The nearest big hospital was very willing to use the money for research they were doing. But, after several years, we were told that no more money should be sent as the research had shown that it was a genetic condition and that nothing could be done for those who suffered from it. They were not even able to give it a specific name. I suppose the only crumb of hope that came out of the research was that carriers could be identified and could be given genetic counselling. The hard fact was that if the young members of the family were all to stop having children the disease would die out in a generation.

It was when Hew's children were very young that I first had suspicions that he was developing Tom's condition. And I was right. Over the years that followed, I watched my middle son put up a magnificent struggle against weakness, disability and fear. He was a wonderful father, and did as much as he could for as long as he could with his children. Like Tom, he lost his balance, and stumbling and bumping into things became normal. Later a wheelchair was a necessity. But probably one of the most distressing aspects of

Hew's condition was that as time passed he lost his ability to speak. It broke my heart to see him, a strong man, still young, needing wheeled about and fed, not even able to express his thanks or his needs. When Hew's death came he was just in his early fifties. My heart broke.

Jesus understood

Inevitably I watched Evan and Ian like a hawk. They seemed well and hearty, but other members of the extended family were not. As Tom was the first of his generation to develop the condition, so Hew was the first of his. Others followed. There was fear in the family. Jesus said: 'Come to me, all you who are weary and burdened, and I will give you rest. Take my yoke upon you and learn from me, for I am gentle and humble in heart, and you will find rest for your souls. For my yoke is easy and my burden is light' (Matthew 11:28-30). How people get through situations like ours if they don't trust themselves and their problems to the Lord Jesus is quite beyond my understanding. Prayer for me wasn't just an optional extra, it was the pouring out of my heart to the only one who understood my fears and forebodings. And going to church wasn't a luxury, it was where I found the support of the wonderful friends who kept me going.

If telling the young members of the family not to have children seemed like a solution as far as medical researchers were concerned, it was not. Just as teenagers driving at eighty miles an hour don't think that an accident can happen to them until it does, so it was regarding this illness. Even those, one of whose parents suffered from, or had died from, the terrible condition, 'knew' that it couldn't happen to them. It might, they thought, happen to their cousins, possibly even to their brothers or sisters, but not to them. So, like their friends, they married and started to have children of their own. Years feel as though they pass more quickly as you grow older, and it seemed to me no time until I was a great-grandmother to several dear little babies, some of them Hew's grandchildren.

It was at a family get-together that I learned what I had feared, that one of Hew's children had been diagnosed as having the condition, but not before she was a mother. Shortly afterwards her sister was found to have it too. She is unmarried. I can't begin to describe my feelings. The only ones who can really understand are those in my extended family who are watching the whole thing unfold in their own lives. And, because it is so hard to face, we don't really talk about it. What is there to say?

The future is in God's hands
I'm in my eighties now and I have a lot to be thankful for. I've had much happiness in my life

as well as grievous sorrows. Like many older people, I often look back over the years and remember. But I have a problem looking forward. Of course I look forward to heaven and to being there with my dear Lord Jesus for ever and ever. If I had not that to look forward to, I would be lost indeed. But, when I look at my darling grandchildren and great grandchildren, when I see the little ones playing and hear them laughing, I can't look forward, for it may be that their future hides the dark spectre of their family's genetic condition.

Much prayer has been poured out on their behalf, and it will be as long as I am on this earth. It is my prayer that they might come to a real and living faith in the Saviour, for if in his strange providence they develop the condition, they will need his help and support to see them through it. I long that, whatever the future holds for them, they might know that reality of the psalm I love:

Those that are broken in their heart,
and grieved in their minds,
He healeth, and their painful wounds
he tenderly up-binds.
He counts the number of the stars;
he names them ev'ry one.
Great is our Lord, and of great pow'r
his wisdom search can none.

(Psalm 147:3-5, Scottish metrical version)

5

AJITH FERNANDO

When Sri Lanka experienced its first of many recent violent uprisings in 1983, the truth that God burned into my heart more than any other was that he is sovereign over history. No other truth has helped me in my life and ministry as much as this as we have experienced waves of violence and unrest in the eighteen years since then. The Tamil race comprises about 18% of Sri Lanka's population. Tamil militants are waging a war in order to have a portion of the country as an independent Tamil homeland. Over 60,000 people have died in this war since 1983. In the late 80s a militant group from the Sinhala majority attempted to overthrow the government and, while no one knows how many died in that uprising, the figures go up to as high as 60,000. Amidst all this turmoil the church has been growing. But this has prompted a new wave of persecution on the Christians, with the burning of churches and attacks on new Christians and the evangelists who introduced them to Christ.

Not every group of Christians has grown during this time. But those who have grown have been characterised by a refusal to give up evangelising and serving the people. Their faithfulness has been buoyed along by their conviction that God is sovereign even in the bleak situations they face. Suri Williams was the Youth for Christ leader in the war-torn north of Sri Lanka for fifteen years. When the war was raging fiercely, and he and his wife and two little children were in a very dangerous situation in the city of Jaffna, we asked him to return to Colombo in the south, which is where he was originally from. We told him that it was not safe for them where they were. He refused to return saying that he could not leave his people at their time of need. 'Besides,' he said, 'the safest place to be is in the centre of God's will!'

God intervenes

I saw an illustration of how this belief sustains Christians shortly after Suri and his family returned to Jaffna after a staff retreat in Colombo. They had planned to take the train on Tuesday, but they suddenly changed their minds and took the Monday train. That night, unexpectedly and without warning, the war started fiercely after a few months of peace. No more trains went up north. If they had not changed their plans they would have been able to remain in the security of Colombo without going to a place of great danger. A few days after they left, I met Suri's mother. I was afraid to face her. Here I was, her son's leader living in the security of Colombo, while her son and his family were in a very dangerous place. Parents have scolded me for much less serious reasons. As she saw me, she said, 'Isn't the Lord wonderful! He knew my son has some important work to do, so he made him leave a day earlier so that he could get there before the roads were closed!' My initial shock and relief over her statement gave way to praise for the courage of a brave lady who believed in the sovereignty of God.

Rescue mission

This belief is what takes away fear from our lives. Satchi, a YFC staff worker in Colombo, went with two volunteers to the east of Sri Lanka for a weekend of ministry. The Indian Army was in the east at that time on a peacekeeping mission, and while our team was there a high-ranking Indian officer died in an explosion. This caused the soldiers to go berserk. They shot many to death that day, including the person who had organised our meetings. Satchi and the two volunteers were taken in by the Army and assaulted badly. They were warded in a hospital with head injuries, and they called us requesting someone to come by vehicle to bring them home. They could not use public transport with their heads bandaged as the situation was quite volatile and people seeing the injuries might think they were terrorists and harm them in their anger.

At that time we had one vehicle in YFC, a brand new van (we do most of our travel on small motorcycles). Many advised us not to take the van as we had to go through areas where the terrorists were active and they were known to grab this type of vehicle. Some advised us not to send senior staff persons on this journey, because if something happened to them YFC would be in serious trouble. But we knew that the senior people could not palm off such a sensitive assignment on the junior ones. During the time of deciding what to do I was so nervous that my stomach felt extremely tight. We prayed and asked many others to pray, and we finally decided that it was God's will that the two most senior people, Tony Senewiratne and I, should make the trip using our new van. The moment we arrived at that decision, I felt as though a huge burden fell off my back. We had discerned that this was God's will and therefore there was no reason to be anxious and afraid. We had a lovely trip to and from the east.

Fears
Of course we learned that fear is a natural response to dangerous situations, and that we should address this fear with our belief in the

sovereignty of God and concentrate on obedience.

During the revolution in the south the government instituted a commission to inquire into why the young people were rebelling against authority so violently. They asked those involved with youth to make submissions to the commission. I thought this would be a good opportunity for us to express our Christian commitment to justice. I gathered our staff together and asked them to give reasons for youth rebellion, then I recorded these observations and sent them to the commission under my name. But it was quite an explosive document, which placed a lot of the blame on the authorities. This was a time when some people who publicly criticised the government had been killed, and I was very concerned that they might come after me too. For about a week after sending that document, I got up in the middle of the nights in a cold sweat thinking that they had come for me! This was a natural reaction to danger. But by addressing that kind of fear with the belief that God is sovereign we are able to follow the path of obedience.

If God is sovereign and working out his good purposes even amidst difficult situations, then the Christian response to such situations is patience. Christian patience includes a positive attitude to trials; it looks for good to come out of difficulties and acts with this positive perspective in view. When the city of Jaffna was being pummelled by shells, the people lost a positive approach to life and this was seen daily on the streets. Garbage was strewn all over, with no one to pick it up; the yards of homes were neglected, with weeds abounding where flowering plants once grew. Suri and Shanthi Williams decided that their home was going to reflect the beauty of Jesus. So they tended their garden with great care and made it into a beautiful place. They cleaned the portion of the road that was beside their home. An Indian army officer once saw them do this, and he got his soldiers to clean the rest of the road!

Birthday biscuits

Once Shanthi's birthday fell in the middle of a period when a twenty-four hour curfew was in force for several days. Food was scarce, and things like cake were impossible to make or purchase. Suri really wanted to celebrate the birthday. With great difficulty, mainly by walking over people's gardens and avoiding the roads, he managed to get to a grocery store in which the owners were living even though the shop was closed. All he could get was a box of biscuits. He brought it home and the family had a surprise party for Shanthi with no guests and only a packet of biscuits as a treat. A generous dose of the love of Jesus made it a beautiful celebration.

This story shows that we can have joy even when things around us are really bad. But there is a joy that is even more basic than this, that we can have even when a packet of biscuits is not available. This is the joy of the Lord (Philippians 4:4). During the revolution of the late eighties, the situation in the country was becoming almost unbearable to me. As a youth worker it was terrible for me to see that thousands of young people, some of whom I knew, were dying. There never was a time when there wasn't a dead body floating along the river that bordered the city of Colombo. Schools were closed, sometimes for as long as six months at a time. For a few weeks the militants forcibly stopped public transport. To keep our office open we had to transport all our workers from their homes and back. There were three of us on the staff who could drive, and we took turns to do this three-hour, twice-daily chore. We had just returned from a wonderful seven-month sabbatical in the USA when I had been able to write two books. I found myself complaining that I was a Bible teacher, not a chauffeur! The terrible suffering of the people was really getting me down.

Family matters

Many were leaving the country, especially for the sake of their children. I had received some unsolicited offers of jobs abroad, jobs which seemed to give me the opportunity to concentrate on the things I most like doing. But we believed that God would have us stay on in Sri Lanka, however bad the situation became. We had, however, to think of our children's welfare. My wife and I decided that one of the best legacies we can leave our children is a happy home. But my moods were not helping us carry out this resolve. One day, when I was in a terrible mood, my wife told the children something so that I could hear (our wives have a way of doing that!), 'Father is in a bad mood, let's hope he goes and reads his Bible.' She had stumbled upon a great theological truth. When we are surrounded by terrible temporal circumstances and everything around us looks bleak, we need to fix our eyes on the unchanging truths in God's Word. These tell of a world that will not change, of a God who is sovereign and who will ultimately conquer evil.

This God loves us and is with us, to comfort us and help us amidst the confusion all around, and to turn even a terrible situation into something good! The security of this eternal, unchanging world of God's programme brings the joy of the Lord back to our hearts. I have learned to linger in God's presence in prayer, or with his Word or with my hymn book, and not to give up doing so until the joy of the Lord returns. Through this means theology addresses experience and challenges its mood of despair; the mind addresses the heart until truth penetrates the heart, yielding the joy of the Lord.

Coping with hostility

We have indeed experienced a lot of pain because of the turmoil in the land, however I think that even greater pain comes when there is turmoil within the body of Christ. I experienced this a few years ago when our ministry faced a huge crisis.

There was a major division of opinion about the way we were going to resolve a serious situation that had arisen in the work. I had always worked on resolving crises using the strength of the unity of our leadership team as a basis for action. Now even the leadership team was divided. The leaders in YFC know my weaknesses and usually try to compensate for them, often even laughing about them. But as sometimes happens in a time of crisis, people were now blaming the crisis on my weaknesses. People I loved dearly were very angry and disappointed with me. I thank God that, though the leadership team was dysfunctional at this time, I still had colleagues and Board members with whom I could share and pray. However, I felt that at this time I was leading YFC more through personal prayer than through any other thing. I learned the need to spend long hours, sometimes whole nights, seeking God's face. Out of this period of pain came one of the most important principles of ministry that I have ever learned: in a time of crisis, we must first meet with God and only after that meet with hostile people. Our ministry springs from the security and joy of God's acceptance and anointing rather than as a reaction to people's rejection. If we react in the flesh when faced by hostility we will aggravate the situation. Leaders need to 'be strong in the Lord and in his mighty power' if they are going to be agents of healing in situations of conflict (Ephesians 6:10).

Two comforting truths that have helped us are that God never permits us to be tested beyond what we can bear (1 Corinthians 10:13), and that with every problem comes sufficient grace to tide us through it (2 Corinthians 12:9). In fact, God often sends us his comfort in some wonderful ways which give us the assurance that he has taken a personal interest in our situation (see, for example, Acts 18:9-10; 23:11 and 27:23-24). Many will testify to the amazing way in which our Bible reading for the day clearly spoke to the situation that we were facing at that time. This made us realise that God, in his miraculous providence, arranged for us to read that passage that day. But there are also other ways in which God comforts us.

An egg – sample of answered prayer
When the bombing got very bad in Jaffna, Suri and Shanthi Williams went with their two children to a school that had been converted into a refugee camp. Suri would lead devotions each day with those staying with them in their room. One day, when he gave an opportunity for prayer requests, Shanthi asked for prayer for an egg to give her little boy. Suri was a little embarrassed, because food was scarce and an egg would almost be a luxury. But the request was made in public and it had to be prayed for. The next day there was a severe round of bombing and a shell fell on the home of a Christian lawyer next to the refugee camp. The poultry run they had was destroyed totally, and the only thing that remained was a solitary egg. The lawyer's wife remembered the Christian worker with a little boy in the camp next door. She decided to give the egg to Shanthi, who was thrilled by the specific way in which God answered prayer. Shanthi says that such acts of God's comfort were a great boost to her and helped her in her resolve to stay on in Jaffna despite the troubles.

Prison ministry

Many of the truths presented above are illustrated in the events surrounding the arrest in 1998 of YFC staff worker Jeyaraj, who was at that time a volunteer in our ministry. Jeyaraj's identity card states his place of birth, which happens to be a place from which many militants come, so he is often arrested on suspicion of being a terrorist. On one of his seven previous arrests he was tortured so badly that he had to be operated on for injuries to his stomach. As soon as I heard of his arrest, I went to the police station around midnight along with a Christian lawyer, armed with a letter guaranteeing that I knew he was not a terrorist. The arresting officer chased us out of the station. Jeyaraj was subjected to torture in the police station, then sent to the remand prison. There he was in a state of deep discouragement. It is emotionally very painful when Christians are arrested for being terrorists when, at great cost to themselves, they refuse to condone the use of violence as a means of struggling for rights.

After a few days in the remand prison, Jeyaraj was transferred to a special prison for those condemned or suspected of being terrorists. There he met another Christian and his spirits picked up. The two of them started a Bible study in the prison, and this became so popular that they soon had to divide it into two studies. Then they began a Sunday service which attracted about fifty-five people each week. In order to bring some brightness to the lives of his fellow inmates, Jeyaraj also organised sports, drama and music programmes and general knowledge quiz competitions in the prison.

Realising that some of the young people there could sit for the public exams, he also helped foster a number of educational programmes in the prison. The inmates spoke Tamil, but the prison personnel did not speak this language. So he began to act as an interpreter and then a mediator when there were conflicts between prisoners and the authorities. As not all of the hierarchy of the militant organisation was happy with some of the things that Jeyaraj did, he was taking a big risk in being obedient to God's call in the prison.

'Thank God I'm in prison'

I will never forget taking a group of YFC staff and volunteers to the prison on Christmas Day 1998. We provided a good Christmas meal for all 800 people there, and also conducted a Christmas service. Tears flowed freely as brothers in Christ from outside and inside the prison had fellowship with each other. Several inmates told us that they were thankful to God that they had come to this prison, because in prison they met God. I met the young man who had carried out the bombing of a military building next to my son's school. I had heard the sound of the bomb, and when I made inquiries I was told that it had gone off at my son's school. It was probably the scariest day of my life. I rushed on my motor cycle to as close to the scene as I could get. Then I ran to the school through private properties, jumping over walls because the roads were closed. Fortunately my son had only a slight cut on his face. In that prison I stood in front of the man who had planted the bomb. I was told that he was close to committing his life to Christ. When I heard who he was, there wasn't in me even a tinge of animosity towards him. Such feelings were buried amidst the thrill of knowing that God had been working so powerfully among these people.

Though there were no specific charges that could be made against Jeyaraj, the case was postponed so often that he stayed in prison for fifteen months before he was finally released. We sent word far and wide the day before the case came up in the courts, asking for prayers for his release. But after seeing everything that God was doing in prison through him, we made sure we added, 'if it is your will', when praying for his release. Shortly before Jeyaraj was released, a pastor came into the prison, also as a terrorist suspect, and he has been able to carry on the good work. Before he was released, the head of the prison told Jeyaraj that he could come back to continue his ministry. On his release Jeyaraj joined our full-time staff, and he now visits the prison often and also ministers to the families of the prisoners and to those who have been released from prison.

So our belief in the sovereignty of God not only brings comfort and strength to us amidst turmoil, it also enables us to keep serving and being part of God's action to turn even the greatest tragedy into something good.

6

VALERIE SMITH

Our baby daughter Jennifer was born at Easter time 1981. What a wonderful time to be born! My husband, David, and I had planned for her arrival with much happiness and anticipation, but her coming into the world was traumatic. When she was born, our new little daughter was blue/ black, her features were badly swollen and she needed to be tube fed. Our hearts went out to her as she lay in her hospital crib, battered and bruised from the effort of being born.

By the time we left the maternity unit, Jennifer was much better and we were beginning to see the shape of her pretty face under her mass of curly dark hair. Every baby achievement delighted us, her first tooth, her first word, her first step. As our baby became a toddler, we watched her explore her surroundings, we told her stories and we smiled at her efforts to tell them herself. At the age of eighteen months she thoroughly enjoyed playing with words, her favourite then being 'Pinnochio'. Jennifer cried and laughed, crawled and walked, played and slept. As far as we were concerned, we had a

normal little daughter and we thanked God for
her.

Jennifer was three years old when the Lord
blessed us with our second daughter, Kathryn.
David brought Jennifer to the maternity hospital
to meet her new little sister, but, after a fleeting
glance, she toddled off down the ward to see the
other babies, shouting 'Bye-bye babies' as she
left the ward, hand in hand with her dad. Our
family was complete and our joy overflowed.

Questions but no answers

The happy family bubble was about to burst. As
Jennifer seemed to have settled well at nursery
school, it rather took us aback when the nursery
teacher expressed concern about our daughter's
behaviour and development, and suggested that
we take her to see a child psychiatrist. All the
appointment did was raise concerns in us. The
specialist agreed with the teacher that there was
cause for referral, but she was unwilling to 'label'
Jennifer with a specific behavioural or
developmental problem. This may be helpful
from the point of view of the child, but it is so
confusing for the parents, especially parents like
us who felt we had a normal little girl.

When she was nearly five, in 1986, Jennifer
went to mainstream school, where she was
regarded as an oddity because she developed
increasingly bizarre behaviour. One day, when

sitting at the lunch table, she poured a jug of water over a child's head. On another occasion, when the school toilets were broken and children had to use the staff cloakroom, Jennifer cried and screamed uncontrollably until a teacher came home for her potty.

The school staff tried to integrate Jennifer, but eventually found that they could not cope. She was taken to see an expert in autism at a hospital some forty miles away. His recommendation was that she should stay there as a weekly boarder until her condition was assessed. Our little girl was subjected to a barrage of tests and assessments, but nothing specific showed up. This was a heartbreaking time for us. Even though I prayed for Jennifer and committed her into God's care as she left each Monday morning, my whole desire was to have her at home. How we longed to have our two daughters playing together with their toys. I felt confused; this was not what family life was meant to be about.

After six months as a weekly boarder, an Education Committee met and recommended three schools as possibilities for Jennifer. Although no definite diagnosis had been forthcoming, one school was for autistic children, but the pupils there seemed to be much more disabled than our daughter. The other two schools were for children with mild learning difficulties, one a day school and the other residential. As Jennifer had difficulty relating to her peers, it was decided that she should attend the residential school.

Sad-hearted

It was a cold autumn evening when Jennifer went to her new school. As David was away Monday to Friday, Grandma baby-sat for Kathryn while I went with our daughter and her new housemother to settle her in the hostel. The building was bright and cheery, but I was not. It was welcoming and Jennifer seemed to see it as an adventure, but I did not. I felt heavy-hearted as I returned home. 'Why is this happening?' I asked God. There was no answer. But if I had not known that God was in control, I think I might have cracked up at that point.

Life at home developed into a routine that became 'normal' for us. David worked away from home, coming back at weekends. Kathryn led the life of an only child Monday to Friday, and of a younger sister on Saturdays and Sundays. And Grandma helped in many ways. She and I asked each other so many questions that neither could answer. Would Jennifer be able to hold down a job? look after herself? keep friends? have a boyfriend? get married and have children? We were full of questions but empty of answers.

How someone without a living faith in God copes in that kind of situation, I do not know. When I was in my mid-twenties, friends took me to an evangelical meeting. I was moved to make a commitment to God, but felt that he could not forgive my past wrongdoings. After the service, the minister explained to me that Jesus' death on the cross was the punishment for my sins. He placed a hymn book in his hand then transferred it to his other hand. That symbolic act helped me to see that God had lifted away my sin and transferred it to Jesus. At that moment I believed. At last I was free, and I began to see things as my Saviour wanted me to see them. I bought Bible study notes and started to read Scripture every day. Life did not become a bed of roses, far from it, especially as I suffered from time to time from depression. But I was living each day with Jesus. And how I needed him!

As Jennifer progressed through primary school, she appeared to become more normal. Her school friends had varying disabilities, but they all seemed to play well together. Our daughter was good at art, did well in Brownies, and enjoyed trips to the seaside with other children from her hostel. She was taught social skills such as sharing and taking turns. At home she took turns with the washing up; in fact, Jennifer was and still is helpful at home. She tries so hard to please. As her primary schooling ended, it was decided that she would come home and attend a local special school for children with both learning difficulties and physical disabilities. I looked forward to this with anticipation, and with apprehension.

Holiday horrors

Although we had seen Jennifer as a normal four-year-old, even though others recognised things were not quite right with her, we had to admit that our growing daughter had problems. If ever we doubted that, holidays served to remind us. So bizarre and disruptive, even dangerous, was her behaviour in one hotel that the manageress politely asked us not to bring Jennifer back. To say that we were devastated does not even begin to describe the agonies we went through on that occasion.

On holidays there were always people who complained about her noisy and uncontrolled behaviour, but there were others who were kind and understanding. If only we could have told them that Jennifer was autistic it might have helped, but we could not as we had no firm diagnosis. We were advised that taking Jennifer on holiday was for her benefit, it would encourage her to socialise. These holidays were certainly not for our benefit; we came home stressed and exhausted. Often the night we arrived back home was the first time we really relaxed since leaving to go on holiday.

Her new school seemed to meet a lot of Jennifer's needs. She quickly settled into a harmonious routine at home and made friends at school. Hostel life had given us a domesticated eleven-year-old daughter, a rare breed! Was she beginning to grow out of her difficulties? That was my hope and prayer. Children like Jennifer thrive on a highly structured, predictable routine, complying with it in a companionable way. This gave us a false impression.

When our normal structure was in place, Jennifer was like any other girl. She was loving and helpful, though she could be slow to understand what was happening around her. Sometimes her speech was, and still is, pedantic and formal as if she had rehearsed it. In a way, she had. Children like Jennifer learn to copy what is said, then translate learned speeches before putting them into other social settings. Their impairment in social skills means that they don't know how to relate social rules to different settings. It is also thought that they suffer from a sensory impairment that burdens them with a frightening sense of being overwhelmed. No wonder such children cry with frustration, the world is such an incomprehensible place to them.

Autistic behaviour

Some examples of Jennifer's behaviour may help to illustrate what families like ours go through. In town one day I wanted to go in one direction and she wanted to go in the other. Jennifer screamed so much that the manager of the shop we were passing threatened to call the police. On another occasion a shop assistant did call the police. They have usually treated us with kindness, and Jennifer knows she can approach a police constable if she is lost, and she has been on many occasions. Breakages have caused real problems too. If a toy broke beyond repair, our poor daughter would run around the neighbours asking for help to mend it. Failing that she would dial 999. Again, the police were understanding. Her propensity to dial 999 for help when things were broken or lost was due to my telling her that the police were friends. This is a good example of how a child like ours is unable to differentiate between the police being friends who could help when she was lost, and them being at her beck and call to help when a toy is lost or broken.

As well as inappropriate behaviour, inappropriate speech has also been a problem. Jennifer and others like her hear comments and remember them, assuming that they are the correct way to initiate conversation. I've been with our daughter in town when she has greeted strangers with such comments as, 'Didn't I see you in the hairdresser's with a towel on your head?' or worse still, 'Didn't I see you in the hairdresser's with no clothes on?', though goodness knows where she picked that one up! These children also have a propensity to repeat themselves over and over and over again, often with their voices growing louder as they go on, and quite regardless of the social setting. When they engage in obsessive or repetitive behaviour or speech, it is almost impossible to get through to them; it is as if the behaviour itself forms a barrier which keeps the rest of the world out. Of course, to the uninitiated this just looks like naughtiness caused by poor parenting. If only they knew, they might be a little more under-standing. But there is another side to the coin. Autistic children are often so appealing.

God's unfelt presence

There were many, many times such as those I've described when I called on my heavenly Father for support. The Lord tells us that he will never leave us or forsake us. While I know in my head and heart that is true, there have been times when I've not felt his presence even though I knew he was there, and when I've felt very alone, especially with David working away from home. My involvement in my local Anglican church and Bible study group have at times been used by God to hold me together.

As Jennifer grew up and progressed through the senior unit at the same special school, she showed herself to be really quite artistically gifted. Her paintings and art work were displayed throughout the school. She also took part in theatrical productions and art groups. Kathryn is more musical. She is learning to play the flute, and she now plays in our church's worship and praise group. Her music also extends to dance, with ballet being her passion. But, lest you think Kathryn is very 'girlish', she is also an Air Cadet and has actually flown a plane! What could be more different than going from a ballet costume to combat gear? Like most sisters, our daughters have their similarities, differences, and frequent disagreements. But, due to Jennifer's condition, it is as though everything is bigger than it actually is, as though we view life through a magnifying glass.

Over Jennifer's school years we saw a number of psychiatrists and psychologists, but none was ever prepared to give us a clear diagnosis, nor any reassurance regarding her future. We told people that she had a communication disorder. In the absence of an expert diagnosis, we did not know what else to say. Sometimes I felt as if it was me who had communication problems, I was so stuck for explanations.

Jennifer loved Guides and eventually

transferred to Rangers. Although she enjoyed Rangers, she was a little out of her depth. It was difficult for her to play a meaningful role among young adults. The same seemed to be the case when she joined the Young People's Group in church. She loved the sessions involving interesting activities, but a great deal of what went on was beyond her. I try to think myself into Jennifer's mind, to work out what situations make her feel uncomfortable or threatened. Sometimes I can't do that, but occasionally it gives me just a little insight into what she is going through, especially in social situations. And my heart aches for her.

Where do we go from here?
David and I are ordinary parents with ordinary concerns for our daughters. As they grow up we find ourselves wondering about their future and working out how best we can help and support them. This was especially the case with Jennifer as she neared the end of her schooling. No doubt it will be the same again when Kathryn reaches that stage. During the summer holidays in the year in which she was seventeen, we took Jennifer to visit a college for autistic people some distance from our home. As it was holiday time, there were few students about. The place seemed hostile and forbidding to our daughter. She cried, and insisted that she did not want to go there.

In December 1998, her psychiatrist agreed to give us a firm diagnosis ... at long last. We were told that Jennifer was moderately autistic and had mild learning difficulties. David and I felt a great surge of relief. At last, after thirteen years of waiting, we knew for sure what was wrong with our daughter. But we also felt full of pain; she was not going to get better, and we were hurt that it had taken so long to reach this stage. Today autism can be diagnosed as early as three years old, and early diagnosis greatly assists in the appropriate placing and education of a child. It would also have made it so much easier to explain Jennifer's bizarre behaviour. We would not have had to resort to such vague statements as, 'Our daughter behaves in a strange way because she has a communication disorder,' or that 'she might have mild learning difficulties or autistic features'.

What a comfort it has been to know that Jesus was totally human and that he, like us, knows what it feels like to be hurt. This helps take away the loneliness, and it helped us to move forward rather than looking back and wasting energy on regrets. Where were we to move forward to?

Jennifer left school in July 2000. She was at home with us for a few weeks before going to Cloverdale House in Sunderland, a forty-minute run from our home in Hummersknott. The house, which sits in its own grounds, is home to several autistic students. They live there during the week and sometimes go home at weekends. A large school room at one end of the garden caters for day students like Jennifer. She has settled well into her new environment and has made friends there. Mornings at Cloverdale are spent in the classroom doing a wide range of activities. Each afternoon the students are taken out to destinations many and varied. The staff at Cloverdale think that our daughter may be able to cope at college, where her artistic gifts could be developed, perhaps even leading to employment in a supported environment. With her need for routine and orderliness, Jennifer would make a good employee.

We have to think of Kathryn too. She is three years younger than her sister, but has had to take on the role of the elder. That has at times been burdensome for her. Bright, beautiful and talented, Kathryn has learned much from our family situation, things she could have learned in no other way. Despite the storms and tribulations that come from there being two teenage daughters in the home, Kathryn will come out the stronger for having a sister who is autistic. What she has learned will colour her relationship with people with problems and disabilities for the rest of her life. I thank God for that.

Held and upheld

And I have to thank him that I am here and able to write this account of our life with Jennifer. I'm not superhuman, I have survived only through his upholding. Over the years I have suffered from bouts of depression, but I have come through them. That is entirely thanks to the One who has held me in the hollow of his hand. We are an ordinary family, yet we are still together despite all we've gone through, and that is thanks to our heavenly Father.

What of our future? We don't know what the future holds for Jennifer and Kathryn, for David and myself, but we know that God holds our future. It is not always easy to remember that, but I know it is true.

7

PETER TRUMPER

The sun had reached its zenith in the broad expanse of cloudless blue; the backcloth against which birds swooped serenely on this warm day. Suddenly, there appeared from the right a faint dot behind which trailed the thinnest of white lines, as if delicately painted by an invisible hand. The speck moved slowly, very slowly, across the 'canvas' heading towards its eventual destination, until at last it vanished, leaving only a white trail to offset the blueness of the sky.

The quiet observer of this scene sat watching, until his eyes gave up the chase, fascinated and scarcely able to avert his gaze. Just think, within that mere fleck – a dot no bigger than the full-stop at the close of this sentence – were several hundred people. The busy crew, the obliging cabin staff, the excited passengers: all speeding towards a destination unknown to him. Who were they ... where had they come from ... where were they going? He would never know. He wondered what they would have thought had they realised this lonely figure, thousands of feet below them, had been watching their progress so intently.

The 'full-stop' had now disappeared. Soon its passengers would disembark, but where? It might be one of the world's romantic cities bustling with excited vigour, or perhaps an exotic clime where palm trees swayed. He could picture his unknown, and unseen, 'friends' walking famous streets, breathing mountain air, lying on sun-drenched beaches, or swimming in warm clear blue/green waters – and, unlike him, without a care in the world!

The frustration of the housebound stimulated a fertile imagination. How he longed to feel warm golden sand oozing through his toes again, cascading over his feet; to splash in milky sea as it sprawled along a sunny coastline; to stroll the cobbled side streets of an ancient European town; to ascend a foreign hillside and admire the mountain ranges beyond: all this had once been his delight, but now he was unable to walk a half step from his wheelchair. Never to walk again, or even to stand unaided! It was a fact confronted on a daily basis, without bitterness, but nevertheless sorrowfully.

I am that man.

The facts

At the time of writing: officially housebound since November 1987; anchored to my chair from two months later. A flight of stairs blocks my passage to the front door (the stair-chair too awkwardly positioned for use), and 'difficult' steps stop my entry into the garden. I view the latter through my study window. Of course, my wife Margaret and I could move house, but at what upheaval to our lives? We could have structural alterations made to it, but at what expense? All this has been suggested by many, my preference though is for the status quo. I make no complaint.

One can understand, then, why the passing specks I watch at times so intensely from my front room window possess such significance for me. The trails they leave behind them etch their messages across the sky: 'FREEDOM!' It means so much, hedged in as I am by walls, as familiar to me as old friends. That is, on good days; on others, as welcome as the bars of a prisoner's cell! The good days though far outnumber the opposition, indeed most days join their ranks.

How it all began
In 1959 I was a twenty-five-year-old theological student, and one Sabbath found me preaching at Abercarn, Gwent. I was preparing for the evening service, when suddenly without warning, a dull ache throbbed behind my left knee. I limped my way to the church, and far from the pain and discomfort easing up, I was obliged to preach with my leg resting on the pulpit chair behind me. Thoughts of how I was going to get to my

parents' home in Cardiff featured strongly.

I had no car in those days, and was therefore dependent upon British Transport, but providentially Margaret, who was then my fiancée, had decided to travel to Abercarn for the service. Somehow, by my hopping and leaning heavily upon her small frame, we struggled to arrive at my parents' front door. By this time, my temperature had risen to 103, and bed was immediately called for. The doctor arrived the following morning. He left puzzled.

From that memorable evening, to the diagnosis twenty-four years later, the pain returned to behind the left knee every eighteen months or so. The pattern never deviated: first without warning the dull ache and the swelling of the left leg and foot, then within the hour the very high temperature, followed by two or three days sweating it out in bed. It occurred at home and abroad, during holiday time or not so, whilst walking, driving, or on one occasion, swimming. 'Red-leg', as we called it, was no respecter of times or situations, and a course of antibiotics was its only fear and our only solution.

Eventually, an extra dimension was introduced. Staggering and stumbling, and at times falling, were becoming commonplace. At first I took little notice, being far too busy in the pastoral and preaching ministry in Pembrokeshire. That is, until one autumn day on Tenby south beach, when my left leg refused to function. My shoe was full to overflowing with sand as I dragged my leg back to the car. Strangely, I drove home without any problem, and was able to walk from the car to the front door as if nothing unusual had taken place. However, Margaret and I could see warning lights flashing.

Much to think about
Soon, the inevitable happened. After a series of interviews with consultants, and the accompanying scans and x-rays, in September 1983, now with a pastorate in North Wales, I entered Walton Hospital in Liverpool for further tests. The information was soon forthcoming: the dreaded MS (multiple sclerosis) was now mine, that 'crippling disease'! The messenger having just departed, I lay upon my bed, thinking. MS! I kept repeating the phrase, like a bride rolling her new name around her tongue. 'I have MS, fancy that!' A crippling disease lay dormant within me, and yet at that precise moment, I could have leapt from my bed, jogged around the ward, done a few press-ups, and jumped back on to the bed! 'Well, well,' I kept whispering to myself, 'I have MS!'

I was struck by the irony of the situation. Throughout my two decades of pastoral ministry, I had been involved with a number of sufferers with MS. I had conversed with them, read the Scriptures to them, prayed alongside them, pushed their wheelchairs, and taken them for afternoon drives. Now, I suddenly realised how little I had known them. How often I had been unwittingly glib, when in my attempt to comfort I had merely quoted an apt Bible text without too much thought behind it: e.g. 'My grace is sufficient for thee' (2 Corinthians 12:9, AV). What had I experienced of their alarms, fears and indignities; their constant need for courage? Very little, but one thing was now certain, I would soon be sharing them.

The grim realisation had dawned. Alone in the ward, with the corridor outside bustling with activity, it was time to examine my relationship with almighty God. Was it in proper working order? It would certainly need to be in the coming months and years. Nothing could be taken for granted; I therefore sought heaven's mercy as at the first, and committed myself to Christ afresh, knowing that whatever was going to happen, however prickly the pathway, God had mapped it out for me. A new ministry had opened up, in which far from telling others that God's grace is sufficient for their every need, I now had to prove it in front of them! If, on occasions, I have, it is surely due to that grace, but also to the events of an extraordinary afternoon in 1958.

The afternoon I kicked the flowers!

Prior to theological training I had attended a missionary college, and had just returned from the principal's study with some bitterly disappointing news. Having informed him I believed my calling was to Britain and not to some foreign field, he reminded me this would mean many more years at various colleges, and possibly as many as nine years of further study. I felt as if I had been sentenced at the Old Bailey! What patience I possessed snapped. After three years training for a secular career, which I had willingly sacrificed for a lifetime spent as a missionary, that door had also been shut in my face. Besides, Margaret and I had been hearing wedding bells, but they would now have to be silenced for an indefinite period.

I left the principal's office stunned, angrily gritting my teeth. The 'board' appeared filled with snakes and, shamefully, I was blaming God for emptying it of ladders. How many Christians have been, and are, in that position, like children wanting (demanding!) only the smoothest of pathways upon which to stroll, yes stroll, to heaven. Yet, it is 'through much tribulation' we Christians enter (Acts 14:22, AV).

An unequal struggle

In an agitated state, I made my way to the college garden where, behind the tall hedgerows away from prying eyes, I paced the meandering pathways between the rockeries. For three long hours I waged a private war against the turn of events (alright, I admit it, against God), pouring out my complaints to him who knew 'my thought afar off' (Psalm 139:2, AV). Like many young men in my position, for whom patience lies beyond the fingertips, I was anxious to fly ahead with my schemes unhindered by halters. But I was about to receive a rude awakening.

In lectures the question had often been posed as to what the cross is that every Christian has to carry (Luke 14:27), and now I knew; humble obedience to the will of God for one's life without hesitation, question or complaint. In fact, to follow Jesus' example (Matthew 26:39), and this is the necessary halter, and those who wear it are privileged to do so, it being the symbol of the spiritual baptism of having been 'crucified' with Christ (Galatians 2:20). Mere words or actions in themselves, however commendatory, cannot testify to the quickening experience, but rather true repentance and personal submission to Christ. If he is not one's Lord, it is doubtful whether he is one's Saviour either. One dare not try to separate the two, although many claiming allegiance to Christ try hard enough to do so – and think somehow they have got away with it.

The challenge was presented to me. Christ possessed a cross, given him by the Father, with which he staggered to Calvary – for a sinner like me. He had 'delighted' to fulfil the Father's will, always doing 'those things that please him' (John 8:29, AV). But was I, even if it meant inconvenience and self-sacrifice? Did I really love Christ sufficiently to reply to that question in the affirmative? Despite hanging my head, I continued petulantly muttering my objections, while leafy twigs and the nearby flowers felt the rough edge of my shoe.

I sought to escape Christ's gaze, but failed, as one after whom I was named had once done, and in my mind I could hear the same pertinent question being asked. Did I really love Christ? Of course I did! But then the Holy Spirit replied by searching the nooks and the crannies (an experience every student preacher needs to be confronted with) when he suggested that my order of priorities was awry.

The truth had dawned. It arrived as a terrible shock to be confronted with reality; that although my love for Christ was genuine, it came a poor third. Third? Yes, that was the blow which injured my pride. My personal desires were top of the agenda, followed by a zeal for Christian ministry and study, and loping far behind was a mere affection for the Lord himself. In truth, my heart was lukewarm, and I was only fit to be 'spewed' out (Revelation 3:15-l6, AV). I was shaken. At the time, I was only four years old in the faith, but I considered myself committed to my Lord and Saviour. That afternoon revealed to me the startling truth that I was not as I had assumed myself to be. Who is? – God's thoughts not being our thoughts. In short, assessed by heaven's values I was a hypocrite. In a very small way, I was beginning to understand how the apostle Peter had felt (John 21:15-17).

Convert, or a disciple?
So for four years I had been unwittingly play-acting, a charge which stung, in the light of my having once been a professional actor! I was in reality just toying with the Christian faith, assuming that a convert and a disciple were the same person. A convert is selfishly anxious to avoid ending in hell (understandably!), but may not just then be willing to enter any further into the Christian experience. For that person, the Christian life consists of Sabbath observance, perhaps merely one service, and possibly the midweek meeting if there is nothing 'better' to do. It may mean little else, apart from the occasional good deed. The soul is treated carelessly, private devotions an option; Christ is present somewhere, but far from the centre.

Again, the challenge was presented to me. Christ seeks disciples, men and women who, from a love for him, will obediently follow close behind carrying their crosses whatever the cost.

The disciple, in contrast to the mere convert, places Christ first over all things, and at all times. His family, and even his own life, must be subordinated. Hence, when Christ had started his final journey to Jerusalem and Calvary, with all that meant in terms of self-sacrifice and total commitment to the Father's will, he brushed aside superficial offers to follow him. People had to be made aware that discipleship entails spiritual toughness. Forsaking all for Christ is what is required of his followers (Luke 14:33). Looking back is unworthy of such a high calling (Luke 9:57-62). I had just learned another lesson to equip me for service and suffering.

Breaking point
In the distance I heard the bell summoning us students to tea, the first time that afternoon I had been aware of life beyond the garden. But I was in no position to heed it. I felt sick in my heart. Shaken, and broken in spirit, I wondered how I would be able to return to the main building and mingle with my friends again. I felt as if the laser beam of holiness had penetrated my soul; a lighted torch had scraped the nerve-end of my conscience.

But still God had not finished with me. Supposing he did not want me to serve him – ever – and intended using someone else instead? What if he told me to break off my engagement

107

to Margaret, or as with Jeremiah, commanded me to refrain from ever getting married? Would I still love him? Did I love him for himself, or merely for what I could get from him? Sadly, there was no doubting the answer. Although I wanted to be of some use to God – a desire which has never left me to this day – unwittingly, I had expected it to be on MY terms.

I sat down on the gardener's rickety old chair nearby, head in hands, tearful. Ministry and marriage had been expected within the year, but now both would have to be shelved indefinitely. Instead, God was commanding me to begin the long and slow hard climb for the third time. I could either go forward, obediently and submissively, trusting him from day to day, or seek my own shortcuts knowing he disapproved. What did I intend doing? Christ was claiming me for discipleship, and preparing me for suffering, urging me to place him first; to love him more profoundly than anyone or anything else. And all this for the rest of my life.

I thought of Abraham. What greater trial of faith and commitment could one have than to be told to be made willing by God to offer up his only son as a sacrifice? Yet, we read that, without questioning the Divine intention, Abraham 'rose up early in the morning, and saddled his ass', and off he journeyed to the appointed venue (Genesis 22:1-3, AV). He had had many more reasons for flouting God's commands than I had, but his faith and love for him were greater than any personal consideration. As Abraham is the 'father' of all those with God's gift of faith, I too wanted to be 'blessed with faithful Abraham' (Galatians 3:7, 9, AV).

The twist in the tale

After three hours 'wrestling' with God, and he with me, I walked slowly from the garden a transformed young man. This had not been a mystical experience, no extra-biblical 'second blessing' encounter. It was far more practical than that. Knowing the hard pioneering ministry I was to be given, and the future struggles with constant ill-health, the Lord had offered me discipleship, and I in turn had offered him myself in a wholehearted and solemn vow. I knew there was no turning back.

As I returned to the other students, keeping what had happened a secret (and doing so for very many years), there was something I was unaware of, because the Lord had graciously refrained from telling me. Unlike me, he knew my experience in the garden had little to do with the reasons for my bitterness when I had entered it, but was in fact a preparation for the long-term. He knew that twenty-five years later, in 1983, a doctor would sit on my bed, and tell me I had multiple sclerosis, and that in 1997, another one would inform me I also had cancer. Try telling that to a mere convert and observe his reaction. But when a disciple hears the news, he thanks God for the privilege in the spirit of 2 Corinthians 12:9-10. It is the only way for a Christian to cope with the 'problem' of suffering.

So, how have I coped?
After being told I had multiple sclerosis, followed by a period of self-examination in the sight of God, my thoughts were directed towards my family. How would they cope? I am sure others in my situation will agree with me that our greatest concern is for our loved ones. We watch them having to do so much extra because of our condition – although they assure us of their loving desire to help – and it is difficult. Making matters worse is that there is nothing we can do about it. We lie in bed, or sit in a wheelchair, while others fetch and carry for us. They share our humiliations and our moments of frustration, clean us up and lift our spirits – without complaint.

Margaret and our four grown-up children were understandably concerned, but quickly adjusted to the new circumstances. They, together with my son-in-law, two daughters-in-law and grandchildren, have been wonderfully kind and supportive. Margaret does not have good health either, but has courageously battled on, having to face up to her own health problems as well as mine.

For the next three years God enabled me to continue in pastoral ministry in an active church, although with increasing difficulty. Soon a stick became my constant companion, as my legs slowly ground to a halt like a rusty machine. Entering the pulpit twice a Sunday was like taking part in a climbing expedition! As for my pastoral visits: many a doorpost kept my dignity intact. It was very hard going.

Then one Sunday in the autumn of 1986 the Lord made it clear to me that I must resign. I did, and when the three months notice was completed my pastoral ministry ended after almost twenty-five years. Yet God still had a work for me to do, and how wonderful that disability need not curtail one's effectiveness in his service. Literally the day after my retirement from pastoral work, I founded an international Protestant work – the Vocal Protestants' International Fellowship – and began editing its paper *1521*, which now has a worldwide circulation.

In the meantime, each year the screw is tightened, yes, but by the One who is in control of it. He has observed me in my wheelchair during moments when exhaustion, frustration and pain have made their presence felt; has seen me grappling with indignity, and more than once (too heavy to be lifted) dragging myself across the floor; has heard me cry out, 'Oh God, help me!', and watched me silently weep in private. How often I have lain paralysed upon my bed, and how much I owe Margaret for her support at such times.

But sympathy is not requested, rather, an understanding of what is taking place during those awful moments. Are we Christians, who have been brought low by God, not the most privileged of all people, no longer the mere spectators of Christ's journey to Golgotha and to Glory, but permitted to touch the hem of his experience; to fellowship with him in his sufferings? (Philippians 3:10). Did Jesus not also experience great weakness, exhaustion and pain? Did he not stagger and fall in the presence of others and, 'with strong crying and tears' (Hebrews 5:7, AV), appeal to heaven for help (Matthew 26:39)? In short, is he not 'acquainted with grief' (Isaiah 53:3, AV), a true high priest, and therefore 'touched with the feeling of our infirmities' (Hebrews 4:15, AV); every infirmity, and all of the time?

Little wonder that in the sight of heaven, whatever the Christian's affliction, it is but 'light'; a momentary 'blip' in anticipation of 'a far more exceeding and eternal weight of glory' (2 Corinthians 4:17, AV). If this then is the route chosen for me along which I may truly know

Christ and be more Christlike, may I 'glory in my infirmities'; even taking pleasure in them. Oh, through these uncomfortable means, may the power of Christ rest upon me!

8

JIM AND MARGARET PRESCOTT

Jim begins their story

We learn from the media that one third of people will develop cancer at some time in their lives, and we all assume we are in the two thirds who won't. At least we do until something upsets our thinking. And that's what happened to me.

My wife Margaret and I are Salvation Army Officers, and from 1987-93 we served the Lord in London. By nature I'm an enthusiast, and energetic with it. That is why it seemed so strange to feel tired. Previously I could keep going, now I found myself having to stop for a rest. Driving had never been a problem, even in London, but gradually I found it tired me so much that I couldn't drive any distance at all. However, before I got round to discussing it with my doctor, we were posted to Findochty in the north-east corner of Scotland. We are Scots and the Lord was calling us back home. Such a move always brings mixed feelings, and ours did especially as Richard and Morag, our son and daughter, were both settled in London and it meant leaving them behind. But that's the nature of parenting, and we left them to the Lord's keeping.

No posting could have been more of a change. From working in the city, surrounded by mile upon mile of houses in every direction, we found ourselves in a little Banffshire village, with the sea in front of us and the hills behind. From the anonymity of the capital, we moved to a community so small that everyone knew everyone else, and everyone knew what everyone else was doing before they even did it!

For some months I put my increasing tiredness down to the move, getting to know a new group of people, coming to terms with a new set of challenges. Knowing that moving house and changing jobs both rank high on any list of stress creating situations, I tried to be patient as I waited for my characteristic vigour to return. It didn't. There was nothing for it but to go to the doctor, and that took a bit of doing. I'm just not the type of person who takes aches and pains to the surgery, I'm so used to them going away by themselves. Some investigations were carried out, but nothing sinister showed up. With Margaret's help and support I just soldiered on.

Postings in the Salvation Army can be quite short, and only two years after going to Findochty we were on the move again. In May 1995 we moved to Springburn in Glasgow, our home city. From the peace of a coastal village we were plunged into the harsh realities of an inner city deprived area. We didn't need to look for work in Springburn, it was on our doorstep. Glasgow people are among the most resilient there are. There were problems all around us, and there were people battling to cope against everything that was stacked against them. Husbands and fathers spent day after weary day looking for work, while their wives eked out the dole money with whatever odd jobs they could find. Grannies looked after children to let their single daughters work long hours to keep them. Of course there were others. Drug addicts and alcoholics, battered wives and abused children all needed the Army's help too. We did our best, but I knew in my heart of hearts that there was something wrong. My tiredness was sometimes overwhelming. Moving about so much didn't help, as each move meant a new doctor, and each new doctor seemed to start right at the very beginning again. I was years into whatever was wrong with me, but I was no nearer to knowing what it was.

A year and a half later Margaret and I received notice that we were being posted to Campbeltown in the south-west of Scotland, 137 miles from Glasgow. From a city of a million, we found ourselves among the six thousand souls in Campbeltown, a move that felt very positive. But people's needs are the same wherever they live, and Margaret and I were thrown right in at the deep end. My tiredness was worse than ever, so much so that before we were long in our new posting I went to the doctor, firmly determined to find out once and for all what the problem was. And when medication did not help, there was nothing for it but to have further tests. After such a long time of knowing I wasn't as well as I should have been, it was a great relief to know that it would be thoroughly investigated.

'Are my results back yet?' I asked over the phone to the surgery.

'Yes,' I was told. 'One is negative and the other is middle of the road.'

My mind raced. 'Middle of the road?' I repeated. 'What does that mean?'

The voice was reassuring. 'There's nothing to worry about.'

But because I was worried, and I knew I was unwell, an appointment was made for me to see a specialist. He arranged for tests as an in-patient in January 1997 in Oban, the nearest hospital where such investigations could be done. These were carried out, including a bowel biopsy which I watched on screen. The interest of what was happening on the monitor took my mind off my surroundings. Although I couldn't see anything wrong, when the results came back they showed early signs of malignancy. I needed surgery and this was programmed for March, which suited me fine. I had work to do before that because February was the time of year for the Salvation Army's Annual Appeal. That's a really important time in the Army, as the money collected helps to fund our extensive social work programme. And the Self Denial Appeal, that ran alongside it, raised money for the Army's mission work and general needs. Consequently there wasn't too much time to think and March came quickly.

Margaret
We are quite a small Corps in Campbeltown, but that doesn't make the Annual Appeal any less work, probably just the opposite. Although Jim was at home and taking an active part in it all, I was increasingly aware of his tiredness. Sometimes when I looked at him, he seemed much older than his age. When the time came for him to go in for surgery, I felt both relieved that the problem was to be dealt with and concerned about the outcome.

Jim
When the early signs of malignancy were detected, I began to wonder if I was one of the third of the population who would have cancer. Memories of my mother flooded into my mind. I was forty-nine, she had developed bowel cancer when she was fifty. Chemotherapy followed her diagnosis, and she lived for another ten years.

Such thoughts meant that I was anxious and very emotional. And I felt as though I was on the wrong end of things. So often over my career as a Salvation Army Officer I had comforted people in the situation I now found myself in, encouraging them to believe that God would keep his promises, that he would never leave them nor forsake them. That was now being tested in my own life.

Although Oban is about ninety miles from Campbeltown, it is not the easiest place to get to. It takes all day to get there and back by public transport. In any case, when I was away all the responsibility of the Corps fell on Margaret's shoulders. She was so snowed under with work that time for visiting was limited. Thankfully she knew that I was in the best possible place. It was as though the Lord had taken us to Campbeltown just in order that I could be in hospital in Oban. I could not have had better care anywhere.

Having often given pastoral support, I found myself on the receiving end for a change. The Salvation Army was incredibly supportive, from Headquarters right down to local Corps, both in Oban and Campbeltown. And Margaret was given practical help from so many good people. Although we had only been there a short time, the Kintyre folk took her to their hearts and proved to be real friends.

Margaret

Living in a remote area has its blessings, and there can be few places as beautiful as Kintyre. It is only when something is wrong that you feel the distance and remoteness. When Jim was in Oban he might as well have been in London. It made me feel for our local friends who make very long journeys when family members are in hospital.

When I heard the result of Jim's biopsy, I was devastated. These things always happen to someone else. Life seemed to turn upside down. The work had to go on, and in a way that helped me, especially as Jim was in hospital much longer than we thought he would be. And there was the journey. Suddenly Campbeltown to Oban became much further than its usual ninety miles away! There was a landslide on the main road and it was closed thanks to many hundreds of tons of rock. The diversion involved a thirty-two mile single track road, which was regularly impassible because cars trying to pass each other landed in the ditch. Because I don't drive, I was dependent on friends giving me lifts.

Life seemed almost surreal. I couldn't take in what was happening to Jim. He's such an outgoing person with so much to offer. I wanted it to be me who was ill, not him. People were really kind. Cards and phone calls came from people I'd not even heard of. Gifts of fruit and flowers were left at the door. And one alcoholic man came to ask how Jim was, and told me that he didn't want him to die. I didn't really think he would die. Somehow my mind didn't focus on that. That was one of God's blessings at the time; I would have found it much more difficult if I'd thought this was the end.

Jim

Unlike Margaret, I did think I was going to die. I suppose that was because of Mum's illness, and death as a result of it. All kinds of things went through my mind. I found myself looking back, especially over our years in God's service; I suppose this was because I felt they might now be coming to an abrupt close. As a very young man, I had felt the Lord's call to full time service, and Margaret had too. We became very involved in Christian work. Ours wasn't an only-a-Sunday-morning religion, and weekends saw us selling *War Cry* in the streets and public houses of Glasgow, teaching in the Sunday School and singing with the Songsters. And our weeknights were busy too. Both Margaret and I became involved in the Army's social work, including feeding homeless people who, due to alcohol, drugs or changed circumstances in their lives, lived in the bowels of city-centre office blocks, anywhere that was sheltered from the worst of the elements.

I worked hard as an engineer with a view to saving for Salvation Army College, but as year followed year we didn't go and the money frittered away. There were all sorts of reasons, but none was to our credit. Many years passed before we were obedient to his call. Because our son Richard was fifteen and our daughter Morag eleven when the Lord's call became utterly irresistible, we discussed it thoroughly with them. Our hearts were thrilled by their response. Recognising the rightness of what we were proposing, Richard and Morag were totally behind us. Suddenly our lives had direction. We were moving, and we were moving forward.

The William Booth International Training College in Denmarkhill, London, was where we did our training. This is residential, and that made a huge difference to our family life. Suddenly we were not Dad, Mum and two teenagers, we were part of a community. Activities were arranged for the children of students while their parents studied or engaged in practical training. Although Richard and Morag were well past the stage of needing babysitters, it was good to know they were safe and cared for. And there were several other teenagers around, which helped make up for the friends they had left behind in Glasgow. Even after we moved out of college grounds into a flat, we still had to take part in all the communal activities. But although we loved college, Margaret and I really struggled with studying. It was twenty years since we had left school, and neither of us are bookworms.

Memories of our first posting in London flooded back too. That had been a real baptism of fire. Apart from all the regular spiritual and social work that the Army is involved in, we found ourselves with oversight of the back-up emergency vehicle. The routine was that if more than ten fire tenders were called out to an incident, the emergency vehicle attended, officers giving whatever support they could. We were involved in several call-outs, including to the aftermath of a train derailment at Purley and the appalling rail crash at Clapham Junction, where many people lost their lives. Our input at Clapham was to minister practically and spiritually to those involved in clearing up the debris, rather than at the time of the accident. We also attended fires and floods. Even Morag was involved, young though she was, especially when work needed to be done that coincided with our Sunday services. As I lay in hospital, there was time to think back over the years.

And I thought of the future too. We'd often talked about what we would do in our retirement, now I wondered if I would have one. I felt the Lord still had work for me to do. He was very near to me during that time in hospital, even when I had a setback. Having been up and about after surgery, I took really quite unwell and had to spend a week longer in hospital than we expected.

That assurance only came because I was a Christian. When I was eleven years old, I trusted my young heart to the Lord. That was when I found salvation, and Jesus has been my faithful friend from that day on. Seven years later, I knelt beside a chair in the vestry of a church in Glasgow, and promised to serve the Lord for the rest of my life. It was on the basis of the faith he gave me at my conversion, and the company he had kept me over all the years since, that I knew he was with me even when I felt alone. And I knew he was with Margaret too, though I was very concerned about the burden she was having to bear.

Margaret
That was a very difficult time. Morag came up from London, then Richard, and they were a great support. Unfortunately they saw their dad when he was at his worst. And they saw me at my worst too. It is in situations like that that you realise your children are adults, when you are able to share your problems with them. In a way I think they felt more for me than for Jim. They knew he was being well looked after in Oban, but they felt I was very much out on a limb and on my own in Campbeltown. But although we had just

been there for a short time, we had family in the town. I became a Christian in Sunday School when I was just seven years old and it has been one of the joys of my Christian life to discover that fellow believers are brothers and sisters, because we are all children of our heavenly Father. It was my newly found brothers and sisters who supported me and came to my help. When I felt alone, and there were times when I did, I thanked God for them.

Jim

Having found the early signs of malignancy when I had my tests done, it came as a great surprise to learn that the biopsy taken when I had surgery was clear, completely clear. I've often wondered since then if God healed me in a miraculous way, and I don't know. My first two working weeks I spent at Brengle on spiritual retreat. In a sense the previous six months had been a spiritual journey, but that two-week retreat helped me consolidate what I had learned, and gave me the opportunity to commit the rest of my life to the Lord's service, however long or short my life should be. While I was there I wrote a song that put my feelings into words. This is part of it:

While life is a journey we're all going through;
There are times on our journey, we need to renew
Our life in the Spirit, our hopes and our joy,
The Spirit of peace the world can't destroy.

    It's those moments of grace, Lord,
    When you come to me;
    It's those moments of grace, Lord,
    When you set me free;
    I'm born of the Spirit, I'm lost in his love,
    Those moments of Grace, Lord,
    From heaven above.

I sit in your presence, I can't hear your voice,
I dwell in the gloom when I need to rejoice;
I look for your glory, I only find fear,
I'm far from my Lord though I know he is near.

So Lord through my darkness
My doubt and despair,
Break through to my soul,
Let me know you are there;
I'll give you the honour, I'll give you the praise
And dwell in your love for the rest of my days.

Four years have passed since my surgery. The
first few weeks were slow-going, but before long
my strength built up and I was more and more
able to join Margaret in the work of the Corps.
But the experience I went through has changed
my attitude to life. In some ways I feel I am living
in bonus time. Each day is a gift, a precious gift,
from the God who created it. And it is mine to

use to the full. The work of the Corps keeps me busy, but the main focus of my life is the Lord. I can only do what I do for him if I keep my eyes fixed on him, the author and the finisher of my faith.

9

ROB HOPKINS

I was an only child, born in England but of Scottish parents, both of whom were very private people. Although they never discussed or showed feelings – or anything else of great importance – I did not feel unloved. My mother thought she was a Christian because she had been christened as a child, and my father, if pressed, as he often was by his brother Robert, a fervently evangelical Christian, would admit to being agnostic. Uncle Robert was full of fun, and showed such a great appreciation of everything. I was unaware then that it was the love of the Lord that was shining in him.

As a teenager I became extremely rebellious and (unintentionally, I think) gave my parents a very hard time. My late teens and early twenties were taken up travelling around Europe with a 'pop' band, making and losing small fortunes and experiencing both high life and low life. At twenty-three, like the prodigal, I regained my senses, returned home and got a job. I also began dating a young lady called Helen. At work I met men about my own age who reminded me of

Uncle Robert, and when I eventually enquired about their exuberance and contentment, they replied that they were Christians. Like Mum, I thought I was 'Christian', but I discussed this further with them and eventually accepted an invitation to their chapel.

Just for me

Some months later, when Uncle Robert was visiting, I told him about my workmates and their chapel, and that Sunday evening we both attended the service there. Although I cannot remember what was said or sung, it felt as if it had been laid on especially for me. Afterwards Uncle Robert prayed with me and I accepted Jesus as my Saviour. Within a year my uncle went to be with the Lord, but not before he had written to tell me that he had prayed for me since the day I was born. Helen never met Uncle Robert, but she became a Christian through the ministry of that same chapel and it's pastor, Ernest Mcquoid, and we were married in our local village church in the parish of Barrow near Chester a year later.

Shortly after that, Mum and Dad moved to the North York Moors, to be close to Mum's sister and brother. The Lord led me into teaching. Helen and I and our two children, Nicola and Daniel, with whom God so generously blessed us, spent almost every holiday there, always encouraging my parents to come to church with us. We had many lively debates about the Bible and Christianity, and it was a really special day when Dad told me that they had both knelt down in their lounge and asked the Lord Jesus into their lives.

All change

In 1982 I was appointed to a teaching post in Plymouth, 400 miles from my parents. Dad was seventy-six, Mum five years younger, and both were mentally and physically very active. But Dad was a pragmatist and he soon recognised that our 400 mile separation would be an increasing problem. We talked about finding a small place near to us for them to purchase. The Lord then led us to our present home which, with a little modification, provided Mum and Dad with a self-contained flat. They soon settled in, attended the local Methodist Church, joined the bridge club, and took our young dog on many long walks. Those were precious years. My parents appreciated seeing us and our children every day, while we had the benefit of a permanent babysitter and an expert gardener!

Unlike me, Dad was methodical and well organised. Tools were racked precisely according to size and type; vegetables were grown in tidy rows, flowers in symmetrical borders, seeds sown at the correct times and crops rotated periodically. Drawers and cupboards had a place for everything, and everything in its place. Dad could lay his hand on whatever he was looking for in a matter of seconds, and he prided himself on his memory. He was therefore probably aware a long time before we were that his memory was beginning to 'fail'. He was then seventy-nine. Within a very short time of each other, a specialist informed us that Dad had inoperable cancer, arising from a problem many years earlier, and his doctor told us that he was suffering from dementia.

We had suspected the latter and wondered how it would affect family life. But cancer made a big difference to the equation. Like Dad, I had a rather pragmatic approach, reasoning that at his age the end of his earthly life could not be too far away, and God had permitted this to be the way forward. I prayed that he would give us the strength and wisdom to cope. Helen asked practical questions about time-scale, treatment and help, while I was more concerned to know how Mum was reacting. Although she was there at each meeting, we recognised much later that Mum did not appear to accept the facts. It was her way of coping. I had seen it many times before when I had suggested new ideas.

'Really?' she would say in a voice that sounded as if she would give the suggestion some serious thought, but which was more accurately translated as: 'Think what you like, but I will carry on as I always have done.'

With the situation that now presented itself, she was in a bit of a quandary. Not that she ever confided her thoughts to us, but we could plainly see the dilemma. On the one hand she always had a servant heart, and as Dad became less able she extended her servant role. On the other hand, she had always relied on Dad to make the key decisions in their lives and to do all the 'man's work'. Now, little by little, he was finding his role more challenging. He gave up driving (because of his hearing, he said), and shortly afterwards he stopped playing bridge, though he still continued to walk to the shops every day and to chapel with Mum every Sunday.

Quiet struggles

Partly because of Mum's inability to share, and partly because we were both working, Helen and I did not see all of their struggles. However, during the early summer after Dad's eightieth birthday, we saw increasing confusion in the garden, with many different vegetables growing in the same rows, and random flowers appearing in odd places even though little labels were to be observed everywhere, as he valiantly struggled to maintain some form of structure. Knowing Dad as I did, that sight saddened me terribly.

I had a great love and respect for my father,

and my prayers at that time were that the Lord would be gentle with him as he approached death. I was led to that passage at the end of 1 Corinthians 15, which reads, 'Death has been swallowed up in victory.' Autumn brought with it significant developments in both of Dad's illnesses, though he did not by then recognise either his physical illness or his dementia. Angry exchanges erupted between my parents as both gave vent to their frustrations. At that time I was not in touch with my feelings, and as Mum never disclosed hers either, we both just soldiered on.

Helen was the one who felt excluded from all that was going on. She asked how I felt, but I was unable to respond with anything more than, 'I'm okay.' There were feelings of turmoil deep inside me, but I tried to ignore them. To Helen, my reply was a rejection of her desire to share, and this was not made any easier for her because of Mum's unwillingness to talk about her feelings. Helen and I had not developed the habit of praying together, though prayer was important to both of us.

Confusion and frustration

As time passed, Dad became even less mobile and sat for long periods, reading the newspaper or watching television. We noticed that he read the same page of the paper numerous times and that he was also becoming confused about who various people were. Mum's frustration was revealed over little things, for example, when Dad once referred to his brother Robert coming to see him. 'Don't be silly, Sam,' she responded impatiently. 'He's been dead for more than fifteen years!' 'Why didn't anyone tell me?' Dad responded. His face fell and he burst into tears. Fortunately his pain was short-lived.

Dad started sleeping during the day then waking at night. Mum then had to get up and coax him back to bed. Although this must have been incredibly frustrating and exhausting for her, she still resolutely opposed suggestions and offers of help. The turning point came in early November when, at about two o'clock one morning, Dad wandered into our bedroom saying, 'There's dead bodies everywhere!' We assumed that his mind was back in the war years, but we were surprised that Mum did not appear behind him to shepherd him back to bed. The reason for that became clear when we took Dad back to their bedroom and discovered her lying on the floor. She was conscious and we gently helped her into bed before calling the doctor. Exhaustion was quickly diagnosed, and the immediate 'treatment' was for Dad to have some respite care in the local hospital while Mum went to stay with her sister, Peggy. We put in place a system whereby a Marie Curie Nurse would spend one night in three looking after Dad. Helen and I shared a second night between us, and Mum took the third.

My memories of those nights are of Dad coming in from his bedroom next door, upset because he was reliving in his mind things he had done wrong in the past. Each time I reassured him with the gospel message of forgiveness through repentance, and we prayed through each of the issues. Helen, who took over from me, said that he slept soundly for the rest of these nights. While I had never prayed with Dad before, I felt able to pray with him then. Although Dad still recognised me, it was as if I were no longer his son. Sometimes he called me the doctor and sometimes I was a face from the past. I felt guilty because I had not built a stronger relationship with him, because I had not said all the things I wanted to, and because my clinical detachment might somehow have contributed to our severed relationship.

Precious memory

Christmas Day 1986 arrived, and Mum wanted us all to go as a family to church. It was about two months since Dad had been out of the house and we were doubtful whether he would recognise anything that was happening. But, when the first carol began, he struggled to his feet and began to sing as well as he was able. Throughout the service he was amazingly attentive, singing all the familiar carols from his childhood days, and when it came to the communion, he walked to the communion rail unassisted. He ate very little Christmas dinner, but in the afternoon he came to see me with a Bible in his hand.

'Where does it say,' he asked, 'that we're assured of salvation?'

We read John 3:16 together. 'For God so loved the world that he gave his one and only Son, that whoever believes in him shall not perish but have eternal life.' Dad's face relaxed and he returned to his lounge. That was the last time he said anything that made sense to us. Five weeks later, he 'left his earthly tent' (2 Corinthians 5:1-5) and slipped quietly away to be with his Lord.

Life goes on

Neither Mum nor I showed any real expression of great sadness, even though Helen tried to encourage us with hugs. Instead we focused on the many practical tasks that lay ahead. However, I believe we did both deal with our grief over the following months as we gradually allowed ourselves to talk about how much we missed Dad. I was certainly able to give thanks to God for the gentle way that he had held my father's hand and led him through the dark valley.

That summer, and for much of the following year, Mum stayed with Peggy in Yorkshire, and when she returned home she resumed her normal activities. As our children were now in their teens, Helen wanted to develop her own career, thus giving Mum the opportunity to take on greater responsibility within the area with which she was most familiar – housework. But it turned into more of a takeover. The arrangement seemed to suit Mum well, but we were losing our independence, and Helen felt she was losing her kitchen.

We put on a surprise party for my mother's eightieth birthday. Helen prepared a banquet to which all of Mum's friends were invited. It was a lovely day and Mum appeared really delighted to have had such attention. We were rather puzzled and upset, therefore, when her best friend wrote to us at Christmas to say that Mum had not mentioned her birthday party in her letter. In March, the doctor diagnosed dementia.

Unlike my father, Mum had no realisation that her memory was failing. Because of her tendency to be dogmatic and to pre-judge, she naturally assumed that someone else had forgotten to tell her things rather than considering the possibility that she might have forgotten. That was just one of many irritations that Helen and I had to bear. Mum began to put things away in the wrong cupboards. We would spend anything up to half an hour searching for lost articles and my mother would virtually accuse us of hiding things from her. She became quite paranoid about people stealing from her. While we were at work during the day, she would lock doors, hide keys, and go through drawers in our rooms, searching for items that she believed had been taken. We tried to be helpful by pinning notices up everywhere, but Mum removed them.

Increasing trials

To add to our problems, we were getting mixed messages from Mum's friends. Her bridge-playing companions expressed concern that she was 'letting people down' because of her poor concentration. And we understood that could well be the case. Yet, when the new season started, and we decided that it would be better if she did not attend any more, the same people told us we were being unreasonable! No wonder that we too were confused.

Two years into this increasing turmoil Peggy died and at her funeral my relatives, who had heard about Mum's condition, told us that there didn't seem to be anything wrong with her. This really did feel like a 'wilderness experience' to us. No-one seemed to understand what we were going through, living with this dear little old lady who always had a smile for everyone and who delighted in helping others, but who thought that we were persecuting her. My teaching commitments meant that Helen was left to deal with much of the problem, even though she was also working part-time. We both felt cornered. It was then that we did what we should have done a long time before, we began to pray together.

Soon we realised that friends from church were empathising and asking how we were coping with the situation. Uncle John came to stay with Mum for a week and went away with a much clearer understanding of how disabled she really was, and how much we were doing for her. Shortly after that, Mum fell while out walking the dog, and dislocated her shoulder. Helen had to spend five hours with her in casualty.

Practicalities of care
Our doctor recommended that we investigate local day-care provision. The nearest centre was not very successful, partly because Mum quite often 'escaped' and walked one and a half miles back home. The alternative was six miles away, but a minibus was able to pick her up and return with her in the evening. Sadly, within a year that centre had to close. Eventually we found a residential home that was prepared to offer day-care, as well as respite care, on an increasingly regular basis.

Because Helen was by then working full-time, I had to take Mum each morning and pick her up in the evening. This meant she needed to be up and dressed quite early. Sometimes, although she said she didn't want to go, we could persuade her. On other occasions, however, persuasion did not work and force had to be used. Even more frustrating were the times when I ensured she was dressed and ready to go, then I had breakfast, only to return to find that she had undressed and was back in bed. To leave Mum at home was not an option as she had no sense of danger. Sometimes I was angry and then she got just as angry with me. Those occasions could become quite ugly.

My prayers on those mornings were a mixture of frustrated sobs, admissions of guilt, and – yes – anger that God was allowing this to happen. But by the time we had completed the fifteen-minute journey, Mum had forgotten the dispute and I had calmed down. A goodbye kiss always seemed to settle her.

As time progressed, I noticed that when I picked my mother up in the evenings, more and more frequently she introduced me to the staff or other residents as 'my brother John'. Even on the better days our conversations became rather shallow, with Mum repeating the same observations over and over again. 'Look at the sheep,' 'Well, I've never seen so many cars,' and 'Aren't the trees lovely,' were her standard ones. If I made any significant statements such as, 'Nicola will be home from University on Friday,' she would respond with, 'Really? Oh, aren't the trees lovely.'

One aspect that weighed heavily on my mind was that I found myself lying in order to keep her happy. When Mum initially went in for respite care, the staff said she really enjoyed her stay so, the next time, we told her about it a few days before. But then she said that she didn't want to go and we had such trouble getting her there. Consequently, we found it less stressful to allow her to believe that she was just going for the day, and then slip her case into the boot of the car afterwards.

Hard decisions

The first time Mum came through to us after she had settled into bed and asked where Dad was, we tried gently to explain that Dad was no longer with us, but with Jesus in heaven. However, this upset her so much that we decided if she asked again we would tell her that he was 'away for a little while'. She was reassured by that and soon forgot her concerns. But Mum's condition deteriorated and month by month she became less settled at home. More accusations of us stealing things, more unsettled nights, and the increasing need to help her with dressing and bathing, all these and many more problems besides, eventually persuaded us to find a nursing home for her to reside in permanently.

Helen had wanted this for some time, but I was torn between 'honouring my mother' and supporting my wife and family. So I had prayed that the Lord would make it clear to me. Our son Daniel's wedding was approaching, and amidst the hectic activity of that, I began to feel more peaceful, and realised that Mum was much less agitated when she was not being moved back and forth each day. We asked for God's guidance to help us find the right place, and to help Mum to settle there. After visiting several possible establishments, we discovered that a member of our church fellowship had gone to work in a home just a mile and a half away. The building had previously been a hotel, and it retained a relaxed and informal atmosphere. It was agreed that Mum should go there on a trial basis because the management was uncertain about having to cope with the violence that sometimes accompanies Alzheimers. But, after just a week, it was decided that Mum was not going to be too much for them to cope with. In September 1998 she moved in.

Generous peace
This was another emotional time for me, picking my way through my mother's things and deciding what she would like to have in her room. I was also worried that she would feel that we

were abandoning her. But the Lord blessed her with peace. Initially I went to visit her every day, but when other things cropped up and I missed a day, there was no indication that she had noticed my absence, so a pattern emerged whereby I would visit two or three times a week. Sometimes Helen visited at other times, and sometimes with me. Nicola also visited at other times, and visits were made by Daniel, and Tamsin, his wife.

Mum is still living peacefully there. More than eight years since she was first diagnosed, God is being really generous with his peace. She seems to believe that she is holidaying in a hotel! 'Where are you staying?' she sometimes asks me. 'Just down there,' I reply vaguely. 'Have you seen Mother today?' she asks. Grandma died when I was two years old. 'No,' I tell her honestly, 'not today.' Mum's words are getting more jumbled, but I still nod and she is content. We can now give each other a hug, a kiss or a squeeze of the hand – whereas at home that just never happened, and the staff marvel at her 'continuously cheerful smile and placid nature'. Though her mind is severely disabled, her Spirit is at peace. I thank God for granting her that.

10

EMMA FARAGHER

I had a very happy and fulfilled childhood, and as I am now only twenty-four, it feels odd talking of it in the past tense! I grew up in Plympton, near Plymouth, with two younger brothers, Richard and James. Our home was always a fun place to be. I have very special memories of family holidays in Cornwall with the caravan every summer, and looking over the family albums I smile as I recall such freedom to explore and develop. I loved school and had many interests and hobbies, especially performing – through dance, drama and music. I loved being a member of the Girls Brigade and Sunday School of Mutley Baptist Church, and the friendships formed there have become some of the deepest and most precious of my life. Sarah, Catherine and Becky seem to have shared every ounce of my past with me, and their love and faithfulness in friendship to me is overwhelming.

My likeness to Mum is at times alarming! I call myself her clone! She and I have a treasured friendship and have always loved spending time together, like peas in a pod. She is an inspiration to me, and her patience, tenderness and faith in God have impacted me greatly. Dad is creative and full of life and humour. He loves learning and being challenged, and I love spending time with him because he frequently encourages me to think about the way I look at life, people and situations. His passion for making music and being in the spotlight have definitely rubbed off on me too!

Family changes

My parents separated when I was twelve. It was an emotional time, yet the passing of years has healed the wounds and I know the Lord had his loving hand upon us all. I have seen the evidence of how 'in all things God works for the good of those who love him' (Romans 8:28), as I now enjoy being a member of a much wider family. My parents both remarried. Dad married Carmen in 1992, and Mum married Michael in 1993. I have the blessing of two energetic younger sisters, Hannah and Ruth, and stepsisters and brothers too. It is great not being the oldest any more!

I can testify to many experiences of God throughout my childhood. I grew up attending Mutley Baptist Church and continue to worship there. I loved the songs and activities of Sunday school, and my only regret now is that I didn't pay more attention to the Bible Stories – I was more concerned with gluing and sticking at the time!! The youth groups were fantastic, and the love and care that was demonstrated to me over those years still blesses me as I reflect now. During some tough times in my teens, when coming to terms with my parents' divorce, their new partners, troubles and pressures of school and relationship experiences, there were some very special, quite exceptional, adults in my life whose prayer and time, understanding and encouragement, have been of lasting significance.

I made a commitment to follow Jesus as my Lord and Saviour when I was thirteen, at the end of a teenagers' event at Spring Harvest. It was there that I heard with listening ears for the first time that God is my Father in heaven, and that he is perfect and unconditional and unfailing in his love for me. I responded to him as he called me by name, and put my life into his hands. At school I was extremely keen to please and I enjoyed doing well. I took 'A' levels in English, Geography, Christian Theology and General Studies, and went on to study social sciences at Durham University, as a member of St. Aidan's College.

Drama in Durham
Durham is a beautiful city, full of character and history. Student life could not have been happier. My years in Durham were full of special

friendships, fabulous opportunities and memorable moments. However, it was during my student years that my physical health began to deteriorate and become a serious problem.

The summer of 1996 was a busy one. I spent some weeks in an orphanage in Poland with a team from DUCCU, the University Christian Union. Then I spent two weeks on a team at the Port St. Mary Scripture Union Beach Mission in the Isle of Man. I enjoyed serving God in these ways, and saw him do many incredible things and answer prayers so faithfully, surprisingly and abundantly. For the remainder of the holiday, I worked for a promotions company as a door-to-door sales representative, attempting to convert people to use an alternative gas supplier!

It was during these six weeks that I began experiencing back pain. Initially it was an ache, which I blamed on hard work and over-straining myself. However, it became more and more of a problem, and I was aware of constant pain. I returned to Durham to embark upon my second year of study, and sought the help of my doctor. Initially I was prescribed anti-inflammatory tablets and later was referred to a physio-therapist who diagnosed a 'self-inflicted posture problem'.

My 'self-inflicted posture problem' did not respond to the exercises I was following. In fact, on 20th January 1997, after sneezing, I collapsed.

My entire body spasmed involuntarily, and it was very frightening. Dear housemates tried every possible method of getting me off the floor and into an easier position. They called the doctor, and later the ambulance, my boyfriend Ewan, and (delicately!) my parents. It was very distressing, as we did not know what was happening to me. I was given an injection at the hospital and sent on my way. But no sooner had we returned home than the spasms returned, shooting screeching pain through my body. The spasms became very familiar, although they gave no warning, and my housemates and closest friends learned how to help me through them.

Unwelcome companion
The pain which seared through my body was to become a constant companion. No medication, exercise or position could bring relief. I grew weaker as the days and weeks of bed rest rolled by. However my memories of that time are surprisingly very positive and pleasant.

God was most certainly and very significantly at work. Once again I experienced the Lord Almighty faithfully working all things together for good, for his perfect purpose. I was surrounded by a swarm of incredibly patient, servant-hearted friends. Day by day I was blessed by visits, cards, phone calls and a shower of gifts. My dear friends stayed by my side through the day and night, and were committed to caring for me. They helped me with every aspect of personal care and as I recall their dedication, their thoughtfulness and compassion I am still deeply touched and humbled. Ewan would simply hold my hand through the hours, and pray for me. Natacha and Sarah joined forces in the mammoth task of washing and changing me. Lizi sat by my side, chatting away, updating me on everyone's news, feeding me chocolates and making me laugh. Steve, Dan and Claire thought of my practical needs, making me meals and drinks, and coming frequently to pray for me, laying hands on me and sharing pictures and words of encouragement. Beckie and Simon ensured I was kept up to date on my studies. Marina and Tracie, my prayer triplet partners, came regularly to pray and share with me, and members of the church family were committed to pray for me too. There are so many others I could mention, whose words, time, care, friendship, thoughtfulness and prayer support was of more value than I can ever express. I thank them, and I thank God for them.

Time, and more time
Because my active, helter-skelter life had ceased completely, my days in bed brought a very unusual commodity – time. I had plenty of time. Although I was very physically dependant on

others – my room-mate Sarah particularly, who took on the sacrificial role of surrogate nurse and full-time carer on top of her studies, I found this time spent with others bore much fruit. I had time to listen, to share and to be still.

My relationship with God began to flourish too. I listened to him – never really having given him the time to get a word in before then! I learned to be comfortable with silence and stillness, simply inviting Jesus into the room and resting in his presence. I kept a journal of all the things God was saying to me through his Word, books, pictures and words of encouragement, and through people around me whom he sent to bless me.

Many people came to pray for me during this time. As they prayed, the Lord, by his Holy Spirit, filled my body, heart and spirit in a way I had never previously experienced. He was in the midst of it all. He was in control. I could never ask, 'Why?' God gave me the gift of faith. I trusted him, knowing this was happening for a reason, knowing it was bearing fruit, and constantly assured that he would be glorified through it. He enabled me to be content, to receive his peace and to accept with joy and a grateful heart the plans he has for me and the wonderful work he was unfolding. I was encouraged to 'Be joyful in hope, patient in affliction, faithful in prayer' (Romans 12:12).

Another special verse for me was, 'Be joyful always, pray continually, give thanks in all circumstances, for this is God's will for you in Christ Jesus' (1 Thessalonians 5:16). I took this verse as a direct challenge. With Jesus' help I could know great and constant joy in my spirit even in the midst of tremendous physical pain. Was I asking for his help? Was I praying continually? This was a major direction from God. He wanted me to pray. I had time in abundance – why didn't I pray?

I began to keep a note of the people and situations I was praying for regularly. My prayer life developed and grew. I prayed aloud, through meditating on Bible verses or poems, in the quiet of my heart, in conversations with others as they shared. Gradually I learned to share everything with him.

Praise the Lord!
My physical condition was victoriously eased on 30th April 1997, when the church family at Mutley united in a day of prayer and fasting for me. By 11 am my pain had changed. The searing, screaming pain was quietened and all that remained was a duller ache. My family, friends and church were thrilled, and joined in thanksgiving to God, praising him for his wonderful work. It was an incredible experience and I had many opportunities to give testimony

to God's healing power and found his goodness overwhelming.

It was later that year, in August, again in Port St. Mary on the Scripture Union Beach Mission, that the agonising pain began to creep back. I tried to carry on regardless and ignore it. Surely if I was serving God in the place he wanted me to be, I shouldn't be experiencing such problems? I managed to conceal the pain, and returned home, admitting it to no-one for fear that it would cause them to doubt God's power or goodness. Nor did I want to disappoint them. I cried secretly and prayed God would forgive me if I had brought it on myself, and that he would heal me again.

I was able to return to Durham to recommence my studies, but after only three weeks it was impossible to hide the muscle spasms and the excruciating pain. There followed eighteen months of treatments, various attempts at relieving my pain. Some methods achieved momentary success, but none had lasting effects. I had three epidural injections, osteopathy, chiropractic, acupuncture, hydrotherapy, physiotherapy, a TENS machine and TSE machine, a magnetic bracelet and a dietician. I believe God led me into these various treatments and I know they were part of his perfect plan for me, although they were not successful in relieving the pain. The scans and discogram showed degeneration of the lowest disc, but the specialists did not see surgery as an appropriate option.

Counting blessings

Throughout these months of unsuccessful treatments I knew the daily blessings of the Lord. His faithfulness to me was so sure. I knew he was working his 'higher ways', for in his Word I read, 'As the heavens are higher than the earth, so are my ways higher than your ways and my thoughts than your thoughts' (Isaiah 55:9). I knew he was answering my prayer, 'Lord, may your will be done.' He led me to a verse from Luke's Gospel, 'Blessed is she who has believed that what the Lord has said to her will be accomplished' (Luke 1:45). Again my time was being used as a rich and fruitful opportunity. I found myself listening, praying and investing real time in people, the people the Lord continually placed along my path.

I was especially blessed by the prayerfulness and commitment of my church family. The leadership team, Ian Coffey, Jon Bush and the elders and staff were incredible. They came to visit me regularly, to share from the Bible and to pray. One of the elders, Maureen Green, was committed to spending time with me every week, and I am so grateful to her for all she shared with me. Her wisdom, prayerfulness and faith in the Lord were invaluable to me, and I am deeply indebted to her.

By the end of 1998 I had deteriorated so much that I could barely walk, and I used a stick and corset to aid me. I tried to ensure I had a little walk around the road every day to keep me from seizing up completely. I never sat anywhere, and could not manage journeys in a car. Virtually every activity was accomplished from the horizontal position – eating, drinking, reading, sewing, writing, watching television, even painting! I was in bed 90% of the time.

It was then that I was referred to a Pain Consultant, who recommended a pain management programme at a rehabilitation hospital. There was a minimum six-month waiting list. This seemed daunting at the time, but God had some very special plans unfolding. My friend Charlotte was in a dentist's waiting room in Essex when she read an article by Maggie Hayward, a lady who suffered chronic back pain. She had made a video, including pain management physio-therapy exercises which had been remarkably effective for her, and which she wanted to share with others suffering severe back pain. Charlotte sent me the article, I purchased the video, and as I began the exercises, the Lord began a very special healing work. I believe God put my friend in the right place at the right time in order that God might guide me and change the course of my life. I spent six months waiting for a place to become available for me at the rehabilitation hospital, but through those exercises there was daily improvement in my mobility and flexibility. My muscles began to regain some strength. The physiotherapist on the video was the senior physiotherapist at Unsted Park Rehabilitation Hospital in Godalming, where I spent four weeks on the Pain Management Programme over Easter 1999.

Circuit training!
It was an incredible month. I arrived there by ambulance, with a walking stick and totally unable to sit. But in that month, the Lord God Almighty transformed my life. The training and assistance I received has made a miraculous difference. There were four other patients on the programme, and although we differed in background and the specifics of our conditions, we all had chronic pain in common. The team helped us regain some physical strength through specialised physiotherapy exercises to improve muscle tone and function – I was even to be found circuit training! The hydrotherapy was bliss, and the freedom of movement in the warm, soothing water was indescribable. We even played games in the water and enjoyed larking around, and we made the exercises real fun. I laughed so much!

An important aspect of the training was occupational therapy, where we were encouraged to challenge our pain. This was achieved through gradually pacing every activity undertaken, initially through the use of a timer. I was encouraged to challenge my physical limitations, casting aside my stick and surgical corset, and increasing my tolerance of pain. I began sitting for ten seconds, three times a day. Then day by day that crept up to twenty seconds ... one minute ... and what a day it was when I could sit for a cup of tea! There were so many other aspects of life that I had ceased to participate in, and through the techniques I was taught for tackling unmanageable tasks, I began to regain some independence and grew in confidence too. I was gradually able to tie my own shoe laces, assist in the kitchen preparing meals and survive short car journeys to the local shops. Life was very exciting and immensely liberating and I knew a remarkable freedom that I never imagined possible.

I have faith in God and confidence in his healing power and believe I have been miraculously restored. God chose to use the health professionals at that rehabilitation hospital to rebuild my body. He spoke these words to me, 'I will strengthen your frame' (Isaiah 58:11), and I held fast to them. In the months that followed, I saw the glorious evidence of their truth.

Enjoying simple things

I have gradually become more and more active
and have relished all the targets I have attained
and enjoy celebrating the milestones of recovery
as they are reached. The new accomplishments
continue to this day. It is a thrill to sit for a meal
with my family. I have such joy in purchasing
presents for birthdays and going to the shops.
The pleasure of being a bridesmaid in August
1999, for my dear friends, Sarah and Chris
Smart, was indescribable. I get a buzz whenever
I climb into the driving seat of my car and am
able to travel into the town freely. I tingle with
pleasure and delight when I enter the church
building at the opportunity of attending services
of worship. And it was such a privilege to be
able to serve the Lord through part-time work in
the church office, as part of the staff team.
Christmas 1999 was so memorable as I was able
to sing carols, eat with the family around the
table, pull crackers, look around the shops for
gifts, and attend all the church services to
worship and celebrate together with other
believers. All these 'little' things, and many more
besides, have meant such a great deal to me in
my recovery.

I still live with constant pain. My condition
and pain have remained the same. I still struggle
with some basic tasks and there are many things
I cannot physically manage. But I am

overflowing with joy and thankfulness for all the Lord has done and the way he has led me through these years. Every day is testimony to his goodness and grace, his power and his strength made perfect in my weakness. My heart rejoices at the faithfulness of my God. Morning by morning new mercies I truly do see. I sing with all my heart, 'Great is thy faithfulness, Oh God my Father.'

I believe the Lord has called me to be a counsellor, and I am seeking to obey him as I pursue qualifications in that field. He spoke plainly and firmly to me, 'Praise be to the God and Father of our Lord Jesus Christ, the Father of compassion and the God of all comfort, who comforts us in all our troubles, so that we can comfort those in any trouble with the comfort we ourselves have received from God' (2 Corinthians 1:3-4). My heart aches for those in pain who do not know Jesus. Because I cannot conceive how they cope and how tough life must be for them and for their families. I long to reach out to them, to share the love of Jesus with them, and the compassion and comfort, strength and hope, joy and peace of the Father. Many people have said to me, 'You are young, you can't have back problems,' and I have struggled to tolerate their ignorance and insensitivity. I wonder how many other young people are suffering silently with pain and are pushed aside, misunderstood, simply because it 'shouldn't be'. Again, I feel compelled to reach out to them, to befriend and to listen. I know the Lord sees the longings of my heart, and my greatest desire is to follow him wherever he directs me. He has guided me safe thus far, and I trust him to lead me home.

Wedding bells

The Lord has also surprised and delighted me in leading me to a wonderful husband. We met in the Isle of Man in March 2000, and knew within moments of being together that the Lord had led us to each other, and it was no coincidence. James Faragher and I were married in December 2000. We have a strong calling by God to serve him in ministry, James as an evangelist and myself in Christian counselling and pastoral ministry. To that end I am now studying theology and counselling at London Bible College. We know that we have been joined together by God and that he has a plan prepared for us as we seek to serve him and give him our lives, in love and adoration of him, bringing glory to his name. It is very exciting indeed!

I was deeply moved when I heard this old hymn sung recently, and the words have been echoing through my mind ever since, as I have reflected on all God has done throughout my life. I know them to be so true.

The King of Love my Shepherd is,
Whose goodness faileth never;
I nothing lack if I am his,
And he is mine forever (H. W. Baker).

11

SANDY FINLAYSON

In 1993 the Chaplain of Tyndale College and Seminary, where I work, asked me to share some of my thoughts in a Chapel Service on what it has meant to experience God's healing in my life. This came at a time when I was feeling awful with the effects of a bad sinus infection, and I was still recovering from a major seizure that I had had a few months earlier. Besides, how could I speak about healing sitting in my wheelchair? Wouldn't that look a little incongruous? On one level I thought I was the wrong person to be asked to speak on the subject since I was, quite frankly, feeling rather sorry for myself. But then as I reflected a little, it struck me that when we need God most we are in the best position to reflect on what he has done for us and what his healing touch really means.

What does it mean to live with a disability? Does God heal? These are questions that anyone who lives with pain, sickness, disease or disability has likely reflected on at some point in his life. They are not easy things to think or write about and there are no easy answers to them. As I reflect on these questions I cannot help but remember an incident which happened to me about fifteen years ago.

Beware of bookstores!

My love of books has manifested itself in a couple of ways. First of all I am a librarian by profession, and secondly I cannot keep away from bookstores. I remember being in a Christian bookstore crowded with people one Saturday morning. I felt a hand on my shoulder as I sat in my wheelchair. It was not unusual to have people stop and chat in this particular store, but as I looked up I saw the face of an elderly lady whom I had never seen before in my life looking down at me. 'God loves you and wants you to be healed,' she said. I must confess that her words startled me, but not as much as what was to follow. 'If you have enough faith, you won't need the wheelchair anymore.' She beamed at me, thinking, I suspect, that she had spoken words which would comfort and encourage me.

Part of me felt angry that she should presume to speak in this way to someone she had never seen before in her life. Part of me felt a mild sense of amusement at what I felt was her lack of theological sophistication. My brain worked quickly as I looked at this obviously well-meaning person. Should I thank her for her kindness? Should I engage her in a theological discussion? If I did, should I deal first with the question of how God heals, or should I tackle her notion that my healing depended on how much I wanted it to happen? In the end, I smiled at her, thanked her for her concern and moved away, suppressing the unchristian desire to run over her foot for her lack of sensitivity. This incident shows that there are many very well-meaning people who feel compassion for those they perceive as being disadvantaged or who are suffering. They mean well, but they are also capable of doing great harm. If I had been calmer, if I had been thinking more clearly, what would I have said to this lady?

Positive beginnings
The first thing I would have said is that God has been active in my life since the beginning. I can never be thankful enough for the family that I was placed in. My parents were people of great faith and determination. Their quiet and incredibly strong faith in God impacted all who knew them. And their determination that they would provide the best possible environment for me that they possibly could, meant that I was born into a very positive family setting.

I was born in the 1950s when medical science was just beginning to deal with spina bifida, which is the particular disability that I have. My parents told me that they were not given much encouragement that I would survive when I was born, and they had to contact several doctors before they could find one to take my case. They were, in fact, told by one doctor that doing surgery on me would be a waste of time because I wasn't going to live. Thankfully, my parents' determination that I should receive medical attention was successful and, despite some stressful times, I survived the critical early days of my life.

The second thing that I would have said to the lady in the bookstore is that God often uses human means in our lives to bring about healing. While it would be foolish to discount the miraculous power of God in the world and in relation to healing, he often uses the gifts and abilities of people to bring about the healing he has planned for us.

For the first ten years of my life I must have spent at least a quarter of my time in hospitals for one reason or another, and it is *only* because of the healing power of God that I came through the various operations and procedures. I am thankful that God planned my life so that I was born in a community where my parents had access to Toronto's Hospital for Sick Children, one of the best children's hospitals in the world. Without the expertise and care of the many doctors and nurses who worked on me and with me, humanly speaking I would not be alive today.

During my early years, time that was not spent in hospital was spent at school and at home. For the first part of my education I attended a school for disabled children. It was a good environment for me to learn and also to receive much-needed physiotherapy after each round of surgery. Being with other young people who also had disabilities helped me to see that I was not alone in the world, and that there were others who faced equal or greater challenges than I did. If my school education at this point was different from what my brother and two sisters experienced, my home life was not all that different. My parents worked hard to treat me the same as my siblings, to teach me their values and their faith. Their expectations of me in terms of behaviour and attitude were certainly no different.

God also brought a number of significant people into my life. I have a vivid childhood memory of sitting with my mother in the office of the orthopaedic surgeon who had done so much to help me learn to walk with crutches and braces. Quite unexpectedly he asked me one day what I wanted to do when I grew up? I think I was eleven or twelve years old at the time. I do not remember exactly what I said to him, but I must have mumbled something about all the things I couldn't do as a result of my disability. Whatever it was that I said to him, he was not happy with my response. He told me very pointedly that while it was true that I had been born with some limitations, God still expected me to do something useful with my life. He went on to say that rather than focusing on what I could not do and getting frustrated about it, I should start thinking now about what I could do. It was very good advice, but it took me a while to take it!

There were certainly times of frustration for me during that period of my life, when I would have to spend school vacations with my legs in casts after the latest round of surgery, or when I was not able to do all of the things that my siblings were able to do. But I look back on my years of childhood with fond memories. The same cannot however be said of my adolescence.

Tough questions

As a teenager I left the security of the special school that I had attended and was integrated into the regular school system. While I needed this academically, I was not prepared to handle it from a social point of view. Along with the usual questions that teenagers have about who they are, and what they are going to do with their lives, I found myself struggling with another issue. Even as the medical profession helped me to cope with my physical disability, a far more disabling problem seized me. I went through a period where I had good physical health but I was extremely angry with God, and I spent a lot of time asking questions. Why was I disabled, and what had I done to deserve this? Why wasn't I being completely healed? I had sure prayed hard for this, but God didn't seem to be listening. In many ways my anger with God was far more disabling than any physical problems I had. I spent a lot of time and negative energy feeling sorry for myself and taking my frustrations out on the people around me who loved me and who cared the most about me. What I really needed as a teen was the healing of my anger and rebellion against God, and thankfully that happened.

Again my parents' quiet faith played a significant part in this. I will never know just how much they prayed for me, how much they pleaded with God to heal my anger against him. I did not experience a 'Damascus Road' spiritual awakening, but rather through the witness of my parents and the faithful teaching I received at the Evangelical Presbyterian Church (which is the Toronto congregation of the Free Church of Scotland), I slowly came to see that I could know peace with God through what he had done for me in Jesus Christ.

Life-changing years

At the age of eighteen, and as graduation from High School approached, I began to ask myself what I would do in the area of further education? I realised that I could not remain dependant on my parents forever, and I was concerned when I saw some of my disabled friends falling into the trap of allowing the state to take care of them through its welfare programmes. Also I was presented with the opportunity that if my marks were high enough I could get special funding from the government to support my university studies. I was accepted into the University of Toronto and took an undergraduate degree in literature, history and political science. It was while at university that three significant life-changing events took place in my life.

The first of these was that I became involved in the work of Inter-Varsity Christian Fellowship, initially attending and then leading a weekly Bible study. This was the first significant opportunity that had come my way where I was mixing with Christians from other backgrounds. Leading a Bible study with Presbyterian, Baptist, Anglican, Roman Catholic and Eastern Orthodox believers was a very positive experience for me. Rather than spending time focusing on what we disagreed on, we studied, prayed and shared our faith in ways that I think encouraged all of us. On a personal level, the acceptance of me by this group as a 'person' rather than as a 'disabled person' meant a great deal to me at that point in my life.

The second thing that happened during my university years was my decision to become a librarian. I had volunteered in the library during my final years in school and had enjoyed it. My love of books had been with me from my earliest days, and as I investigated possible career opportunities, the one that held the most appeal was librarianship. This meant two more years of university education after my initial degree, but my time in graduate school proved to be well worth the time and effort.

By far the most significant event in my time at university was my meeting and falling in love with my wife Linda. I was working as a volunteer in the library where Linda worked, and we were assigned to work on a special project together. Neither of us was looking to find a spouse at this point in our lives, but what began as two people working together on a project slowly developed into a friendship and into the 'library's romance'. When we were married in 1982 most of the library staff were present at our wedding. Linda more than anyone else has helped me to come to terms with my disability.

Encouragements and blessings

Linda's unconditional love, support, and encouragement have been an enormous blessing to me and I can never thank God enough for her, or her enough for all she has done for me.

We have lived and worked in two very different parts of Canada. For the first nine years of our married lives we lived in the prairie province of Saskatchewan, where I worked at the university and Linda worked at the public library. Then, in 1991, we had the opportunity to move back to Toronto, where I am currently the Library Director of Tyndale College and Seminary, Canada's largest evangelical seminary. Linda divides her time now between part-time library work, freelance writing and keeping track of our son Ian and me, which is a full-time job by itself!

It was in 1989, during our time in Saskatchewan, that God brought Ian into our family. When we adopted him at the age of four months, he turned our world upside down and it has never been quite the same since! Having waited five years on the adoption waiting list, we had twenty-four hours notice of his arrival! A number of urgent challenges faced us, including the quick acquisition of all the things you need when a baby suddenly arrives. We were so thankful for our church family, who helped enormously in those first few weeks. I well remember the strange looks we got from folk when they saw our parade when we went out for a walk with Ian. Linda pushed me in my wheelchair, and I in turn pushed Ian in his baby carriage. In his own way, Ian has become a real advocate for the handicapped, expressing, as he does, indignation when I can't get into a building because there is not a proper ramp, or when someone illegally parks in a designated disabled parking spot!

Thoughts on healing

There are a number of lessons that the Lord has taught me about the whole area of healing in my life that I think are worth sharing. Firstly, and most painfully for me, part of healing is being able to say, 'Not my will but yours be done.' We are told we can ask for healing, but we need to recognise that we are dealing with the Great Physician who does all thing well, according to his plans and purposes and not ours. Like Job, we need to be able to say, 'I know that you can do all things, no plan of yours can be thwarted' (Job 42:2). In response to the well-meaning lady in the bookstore, I can truthfully agree that God has the power to bring about whatever form of healing in my life that he may choose. I also need to recognise that he will work when, where, and how he pleases.

Secondly, I have sometimes had a much too materialistic view of healing. I sometimes have reduced God to a kind of super-doctor who is called on when the medical profession seems to be floundering. I am learning to commit all of the areas of brokenness in my life to him, trusting that he will do what is best for me and, more importantly, what is best for his kingdom. This is of course much easier to say than it is to put into practice. But I really do believe that everyone needs to commit all of the difficulties of life to God and seek to leave them with him for him to solve, in his way and in his time.

Thirdly, one of the things that many people with disabilities struggle with is a poor self-image. Let's face it, we are a 'visible minority' to use the politically correct term, and that very visibility can make us feel self-conscious. Gaining a proper self-image is a gift from God, and he has granted me that gift largely through the love and support of my wife and the help of family and friends.

A colleague at work apologised to me recently for scheduling a meeting at a location that was not wheelchair accessible. When he phoned to apologise, he said he had forgotten that it would be a problem for me, because he didn't see my wheelchair any more. While it meant I had to use my crutches to climb stairs to get to the meeting, the fact that he saw me as a person and not as a disabled person meant a great deal to me. It may seem odd, but incidents like this one have been good for me and have helped me to feel better about myself.

Fourthly, as part of my growth in faith and grace, I have very gradually come to an understanding of healing that goes far beyond the physical. To be sure, God can and has healed sickness in my life, but more importantly God continues to heal my whole person. And any ability that I have to cope with my physical disability, is a healing gift from God. Yes, there are still lots of times when I wish things were different, but God by his grace continues to work in this area of my life.

Finally, I need to learn to place healing in its proper context. We need to be still, and *know* that God is God. We need to wait for God to act; and when he does, we then need to live our lives as acts of praise for what he has done. My favourite chapter in the Bible is Isaiah 40. In this chapter God's people were feeling sorry for themselves because they felt that he had abandoned them. God asks them the question, 'Why do you say, O Jacob, and complain, O Israel, "My way is hidden from the LORD; my cause is disregarded by my God"?' (v. 27). God very pointedly tells them that this is not the case, and then gives them a formula for leading a faithful life for him. In verses 30 and 31 the people are told this: 'Even youths grow tired and weary, and young men stumble and fall; but those who hope in the LORD will renew their strength. They will soar on wings like eagles; they will run and not grow weary, they will walk and not be faint.'

Walking with God

The key words in these verses are hope, weary and walk. By the grace of God I have had to learn that regardless of the challenges I face, I am called to live a life that is characterised by hope; hope in God, hope that he will keep his promises. I also need to continue to recognise that there are times when I will be weary, particularly when sickness, disability or stress get the better of me. But this weariness must never gain the ultimate victory in my life. Rather, I need to walk with God, doing the things I am called to do and responding to the challenges I face. If by his grace I can do these things, I can take God at his word that I can run and not grow weary, that I can walk and not faint.

12

EFFIE LAMONT

My primary school days were happy days. Mother was the teacher in the one teacher school I attended in Strathspey and my sister, brother and I were amongst the dozen pupils. We had lots of fun and escapades in the countryside. It was during the summer term of my last year in primary that my mother told us that our school was to be temporarily closed because she had to go into hospital for an operation and that we would be going to the nearest school five miles away. I already knew my mother was unwell and I felt an uneasiness about it. Our father appeared very upset. I had never seen him in tears before. The weeks in our new school were difficult for me. My work deteriorated as I was just unable to cope with the bigger school and my mother in hospital.

I remember asking God to let Mother get better, even for a year. That seemed a long time then. I must have gathered that it was unlikely she would recover completely. She did get better and she resumed teaching in August, but a year later she became unwell again. It was then that I recalled that I had prayed for a year of good health for her. That made quite an impact on me. Mother's health gradually deteriorated as her cancer progressed. She died on 16th September, 1953. I was thirteen, my sister fifteen, and my brother eleven.

A godly example

The devastation of that day remains very clear in my mind. Father told us that our mother had died in the night. I remember my brother asking if he could see her and my heart ached for him. I had my mother for just thirteen years, but they were precious and valuable years. It was her teaching, and above all her example, that led me to God. How I loved the picture she had on the classroom wall, a picture of Jesus with children on his knee and others around him. Underneath was the text, 'Suffer the little children to come unto me and forbid them not for of such is the kingdom of heaven.' I was drawn gently to Jesus as I identified with these little ones, and I learned to carry all my childhood worries to him in prayer. Such was Mother's example and God's goodness, that I can't actually remember a time when I did not pray and experience his answers. Some months after my mother died I was given the wonderful assurance that I was safe in God's keeping. What a relief and joy it was to be assured that everything that happened to me was in God's hands and no one could change that.

Understandably our father was very broken after Mother's death and he appeared unable to talk about her. It was just too painful a subject for us all, and I cried only in private. I know now it would have been much better for us to have talked and wept with one another. Instead each of us bore our grief and pain alone. But life had to go on and time did help to heal.

After school I went to teacher training college in Edinburgh, and in 1960, in Inverness, my teaching career began.

God's good gifts

Several years later I met Calum, who was to become my husband. Our whirlwind romance was a very exciting time for us both. I felt fulfilled and happy, we were deeply in love. Our first date was in July 1973. We were engaged that November, married the following April, and made our home in Glenelg. On 17th June, 1975 God blessed us with a lovely baby boy, Peter Martin. He brought us much joy. Before any time seemed to have passed at all, Peter was a happy, outgoing toddler with a great sense of fun and an adventurous spirit.

The following year there was more excitement as I was expecting twins. Eight weeks before they were due I had to go into hospital. There was the obvious worry of leaving Peter, not to mention the practicalities of his care. As

Calum was tied up with work, Peter stayed with my brother John, his wife Bridget and their two young children, Jane and Andrew. He settled in well and had plenty of love and attention from everyone, with, I think, a double dose of both from Andrew. The twins were born on 27th February, 1977, brothers for Peter. We called them Ronald and Donald. There was a happy homecoming early in March. It was wonderful being all together!

Grief indescribable

But just eight weeks later, on Friday 22nd April, we experienced the darkest day of our lives. I let Peter out to play mid-morning in our securely fastened garden grounds. After feeding the babies I called for him, but there was no response. Our own search proved fruitless and a local search was organized. The memory of the search was, and still is, indescribably painful. Some time elapsed before Calum came home, and I knew from his face that the news was not good. It could not have been worse. Peter had been found face down in the river, having been carried downstream quite a bit from our home. Calum was nearby when Peter was found and he carried him up to the road where he was met by Dr. MacInnes, our family doctor, who tried mouth to mouth resuscitation. Although she could not find a pulse, Peter was rushed to hospital where he was pronounced dead on arrival. How often I had read these words in the paper without too much feeling. The next day I read them about my own wee boy. How differently I reacted then, and I still react when I read them of others now.

We managed to establish that Peter had squeezed out under the garden fence, where the dogs had scraped away earth, because we found his little footmarks in the soil. The river was in spate and he obviously made straight for it. He was a very strong little boy and as fast as a hare. Before it was confirmed that Peter was dead I found myself saying that I'd be thankful if I got him back even for a little while, even supposing he was brain damaged. I just longed to hold him in my arms and cuddle him one last time. But that was not to be. Peter's remains were brought to the house later that afternoon. He looked so beautiful. In my heart I wished I could just keep him like that. I even said to Calum, 'We could have him embalmed.'

The following Monday we had Peter's funeral from our house. The only part of the service I remember was when the minister, Rev. K. Smith, read the words of 2 Samuel 12:23: 'He shall not come to me but I shall go to him.' These words were my comfort. Sometimes it is the simple words that help most, as when a friend reminded me that I had had a happy home, and I still had a happy home. Many a day that kind observation helped me. Often I thought it would not have been so hard if an illness had taken Peter, if I had been able to kiss him goodbye. Inevitably at times I blamed myself for what happened. There were all the 'if onlys'. But each time I thought 'if only I had not let him out', I knew it was wrong, because all things are in God's control. Peter's short life, his birth and his death were, in a way I cannot understand, part of God's plan. Although that was a comfort and enabled me to stop blaming myself, the pain was still very real. Sometimes I thought my heart would literally break. There was the day when we got photos back of Peter and his new brothers. That was heart rending.

Picking up the pieces

I often felt too numb to pray or get near to God, yet I never doubted he was with me although I could not feel his presence. Our hearts were aching for ourselves and for each other, and in trying to help one another we helped ourselves. I remember thinking that I'd never smile again, but I did. And I drew encouragement from people I knew who had had a similar experience and still found happiness in life. Counting our blessings helped too, and we had many, not least our infant sons. The babies had to be looked after and their care filled my days. They were my therapy although they could never replace Peter, just as they could never be replaced themselves. Each child is utterly unique. But having gone through the experience of losing a child, I lived in fear of something happening to Ronald or Donnie. Seven years later my father died but, although I felt his death deeply, it was not to be compared with the loss of my child.

The trip of a lifetime

Calum and I had much to thank God for over the years, and it was with that in mind that we celebrated our silver wedding anniversary in April 1999. As a special holiday to mark our twenty-five years together we booked a trip to the Holy Land. Calum had always wanted to go there. We left home on the evening of Monday, 11th October, staying that night with Christine, Calum's sister, in Culloden. The following day began at Inverness's Dalcross Airport, and ended when we arrived in our hotel on the Mount of Olives in Jerusalem, tired but full of anticipation. Our tour group was made up of Scottish Christians.

The following evening, although we had spent the day visiting many historical sites, Calum said he would like to have seen even more of the places Jesus had been. In the late evening my husband complained of chest pains, but they eased off and he slept well. The next morning he was better. However, as we had been warned that it was to be a very hot and tiring day, he decided to stay in the hotel. He was very happy for me to go, which I did. That day my friends and I walked the way of the cross. We had already visited the site of Jesus' trial, but walking that route and hearing of the suffering of Jesus brought home to me in a new way the terrible agonies he endured. We also visited the Garden Tomb. Our tour leader reminded us that the tomb was empty, that Jesus was alive, and that he dwelt in the hearts of his people.

When we got back that evening Calum was feeling better and a bit disappointed that he had missed out. But he was able to join us the following day as we went to the Jewish holocaust memorial, various churches and a school. The day ended at the shepherds' field near Bethlehem, a visit that Calum enjoyed. During the evening he did not feel too well but by bedtime he was better.

Little did I realize as we spoke together before going to bed that my husband would not speak to me again on this earth. I am so thankful for that last conversation. We expressed our love for each other, and Calum said how thankful he was for the boys. With hindsight it was like a farewell speech.

Worst moment

At twenty minutes to two in the morning I woke with Calum making a strange sound. My very worst moment was probably when I realised his condition. He was unable to speak and had a strange look in his eyes. Our group was all in one corridor. Frantically I knocked on their doors and within minutes several of our friends were in the room. Help was summoned and, when it came, the paramedics were accompanied by armed soldiers. I went with Calum in the ambulance to Hadassah Hospital, about forty-five minutes from our hotel. Sandy Finlay, our leader, and Margaret Fraser, another member of the group, followed us in a taxi. I was very thankful to God for them.

While Calum was to be given a brain scan, we three were sent out of the room. A few minutes later the doctor came back for me. He said they could not get Calum to keep his head still. I went in, held his head, and told him to try and keep still. He immediately recognised my voice and I felt thankful that he knew I was with him. That is a moment I treasure. Calum stayed still and the scan was done. The diagnosis was as I had feared – a massive stroke. Later in the day another doctor emphasized to me the severity of the stroke, explaining that my husband's speech and understanding would be affected. I felt a glimmer of hope, at least they were speaking of a future. I thought if only I got him home to look after him, I'd be so thankful that I would not mind about his handicaps.

As I sat at his bedside I prayed that I would just take one moment at a time, and I felt wonderfully enabled to do this. When I was with Calum I was remarkably calm. He held my hand very tightly and responded in little ways, although his eyes were shut apart from occasional moments. My heart simply over-flowed with love for him. Several of the group offered to stay with me that day but I did not want them to miss their planned trip. I am glad now that they all went, as the time Calum and I had together was very precious. When I returned to the hotel quite late that evening I expected the others to be out, but Margaret was waiting for me. What a help it was to have someone to whom I could pour out my grief. It was very easy to do this with the group as they went through it all with me.

The presence of the Lord

The following morning was Sunday, and my situation fully dawned on me as I walked into the hospital. I was in a foreign land. Calum lay in hospital unable to communicate with me, and my family was far away.

Suddenly I remembered that this was the ground on which Jesus had actually walked, and the land in which he had performed many miracles. I knew my Lord understood my situation and cared for me in my trouble. At that moment I was aware of him drawing near to me.

The hours of the acute period were passing and my hope rose just a little. The main thing was that Calum did not take a second stroke or deteriorate in that time. A few of our group came up to the hospital that afternoon and, with them around me, I almost felt we were back at home. A lady visiting the patient in the next bed told me she was an American Jewish Christian. She offered me her house to stay in as she was going away and our group were moving on. But I was not to be left alone. Catherine Chambers felt God had laid it upon her to stay, and nothing would make her leave. I knew that by remaining with me she was giving up quite a lot, as was her husband Harry who went on without her, but I was never made to feel that was a problem. As the hours passed uneventfully, my hopes for Calum's recovery began to mount.

The following morning I said a tearful farewell to my good friends as they left, and I thanked God that Catherine was with me. When we went to the hospital, we found Calum less responsive. I prayed. Telling myself that he was in a deep sleep, I delayed seeing a doctor, afraid of what he might say. Finally I plucked up courage, only to be told that my husband's condition had deteriorated. I fainted. Early in the evening the doctor told me that Calum's brain stem was dead and that he would die quite soon. At twenty minutes to nine that evening, Calum passed peacefully into the presence of the One who had died for him, and to whom he had committed his life many years before. Even in the presence of death, I recalled how Calum could never speak of Jesus without tears in his eyes and without his lips trembling. I was thankful that Jesus was so precious to him.

Called home to glory
Only days before, I had walked the way of the cross and visited the Lord's empty tomb. That day held special significance for me, as the terrible sufferings of our Lord came home to me as never before, as I realised what he had gone through for sinners. Now, at the deathbed of my dearest one, I saw the relevance of Jesus' suffering. Through what the Lord did on the cross, Calum passed into eternity with the sure and certain hope of spending it with Jesus.

There were the inevitable arrangements to be made and I did not know where to turn. That evening a missionary couple, who had been contacted by a friend of mine, joined us. Carol, who is English but a fluent Hebrew speaker, took over some of the practicalities such as the death certificate. Then there was the phone call I dreaded making to Ronald and Donnie to tell them that their dad was dead. I had warned them earlier in the evening that his condition had deteriorated. How I yearned to be with them as I told them.

It was midnight when Catherine and I got to our hotel. The next day we went from office to office making arrangements, sometimes speaking through an interpreter. Once we got things sorted out we went to Galilee to join the others. Meeting again was a very emotional experience. Just one week before, we had all met in Dalcross Airport, full of excitement and anticipation. How different things were now. But even in my grief and turmoil I felt there was a special peace beside Lake Galilee. Jesus, who had calmed the storm on the lake, calmed the storm in my heart by showing me his love and caring for me through the love of his people. They were his arms supporting me in my grief.

Sad reunion

Two days later we left Galilee for home, a journey I was dreading. Calum and I looked forward to that trip together, now I was going home without him. The authorities in Israel said the remains could take from three to ten days to be returned to Scotland, and there was always a nagging fear that there could be a hitch. But I saw God's hand in the circumstances that surrounded me, and I felt that the Lord who had helped me thus far would not fail me now. We arrived in Dalcross at about 10pm. My sister Anne met me at the airport and I stayed that night with her in Inverness. This was a break before arriving home and it was a comfort to be with her. The following morning Ronald and Donnie arrived. It was a poignant meeting but I was so thankful to be back with them. We sat and wept and talked over the details of their dad's illness and death. I explained to them that it was important that we talked about it and that we continued to talk about their dad. I recalled my own situation when my mother died.

Ronald and Donnie had had a message that the remains would be back in Glasgow by Saturday morning and home later that day. We travelled to Glenelg that afternoon. Arriving at the house and coming in was the hardest part of the whole journey, being met by the dogs Calum loved, going into our bedroom, seeing the clothes he had taken off on the Monday before we left just as he had laid them on the chair. These small things were harder than some of the major things I had to face.

We arranged the funeral for the following Tuesday. As the morning wore on and friends started arriving at the house I was so overwhelmed and felt I could not face it. One very moving moment was arriving at the church and seeing so many cars. It was as if it dawned on me anew that this was indeed my husband's funeral. The church was packed with an overflow outside. Rev. R. Mackenzie paid a very fine tribute to Calum. My sister stayed with us for a week, then we were a week on our own before Christine, Calum's sister, came to be with us. It was a big help and comfort to have their company, but it was when I was on my own that I really let my grief out. Over the next months I shed many tears and sometimes the sense of loss overwhelmed me.

Moving on

I did not return to my teaching job in the local school until the week before the school broke up for the Christmas holidays. That was hard, but it was a big step in moving forward. I found being with the children therapeutic. It touched me when one little one asked me if I was sad when Mr. Lamont died. I felt that even these little ones understood. And I recalled a similar situation after Peter died. My nephew Andrew, who was on holiday with us the summer after we lost our son, told us he felt sad because he was thinking about Peter. That did not upset us, rather it comforted us and drew us to the little one who was also experiencing grief. As we tried to comfort him, we comforted ourselves.

There are things I hope I have learned about

bereavement. I know now that the bereaved person very likely wants to talk about the loved one they have lost, and to talk about how they feel the loss. I don't think we can ever lose someone we love without some regrets. No matter how much we loved or how much we did together, we feel we could have done more. Through all the suffering I trust God has made me more aware of others' sufferings and given me new priorities. As I sat at Calum's bedside, knowing that he was soon to leave everything behind – myself, his sons and everything he held dear in this life – I realized afresh that what matters most in life is knowing Jesus, the One who suffered so much for us, and whose suffering had so recently been brought before us.

I look forward to a glorious reunion one day with my loved ones. Then all who have gone to glory, and those here who have already trusted in Jesus or who will yet do so, will be reunited with the Lord. And that wonderful reunion with him and with them will be forever and ever.